Platonic Occasions

Dialogues on Literature, Art and Culture

Richard Begam & James Soderholm

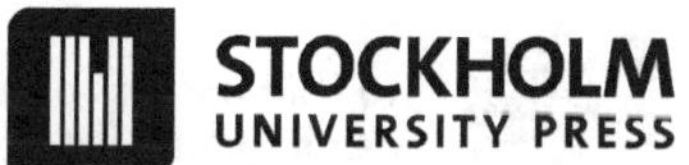

Stockholm English Studies 1

Published by Stockholm University Press
Stockholm University
SE-106 91 Stockholm, Sweden
www.stockholmuniversitypress.se

ORCID: Richard Begam: 0000-0001-5411-8272,
James Soderholm: 0000-0003-0477-3636

Supporting Agency (funding): Department of English, Stockholm University

First published 2015
Cover Illustration: Wassily Kandinksy, *Blue*, 1922
Reproduced by permission of the Norton Simon Museum (The Blue Four Galka Scheyer Collection), Pasadena, California
Cover designed by Janeen Barker

Stockholm English Studies (Online) ISSN: 2002-0163

ISBN (Paperback): 978-91-7635-000-3
ISBN (PDF): 978-91-7635-003-4
ISBN (EPUB): 978-91-7635-002-7
ISBN (Kindle): 978-91-7635-001-0

DOI: http://dx.doi.org/10.16993/sup.baa

Suggested citation:
Begam, R. and Soderholm, J. 2015. *Platonic Occasions: Dialogues on Literature, Art and Culture*. Stockholm: Stockholm University Press. DOI: http://dx.doi.org/10.16993/sup.baa. License: CC-BY-NC-ND.

To read the free, open access version of this book online, visit http://dx.doi.org/10.16993/sup.baa or scan this QR code with your mobile device.

Stockholm English Studies

Stockholm English Studies (SES) is a peer-reviewed series of monographs and edited volumes published by Stockholm University Press. SES strives to provide a broad forum for research on English language and literature from all periods. In terms of subjects and methods, the orientation is also wide: language structure, variation, and meaning, both spoken and written language in all genres, as well as literary scholarship in a broad sense. It is the ambition of SES to place equally high demands on the academic quality of the manuscripts it accepts as those applied by refereed international journals and academic publishers of a similar orientation.

Titles in the series

1. Begam, R. and Soderholm, J. 2015. *Platonic Occasions: Dialogues on Literature, Art and Culture*. Stockholm: Stockholm University Press. DOI: http://dx.doi.org/10.16993/sup.baa

This book is for

Christiaan Marie Hendrickson

&

Janeen Barker

Contents

Illustrations viii
Acknowledgments ix
Introduction x

PART ONE: ART AND AESTHETICS

Flaubert's Hat Trick, Or The Pleasures of Banality 3
The Dysfunction of Criticism at the Present Time 18
The Grapes of Zeuxis: Representation in the Arts 35

PART TWO: EVIL, DEATH, LOVE, POLITICS

The Art of Darkness 59
Let's Hang Ourselves Immediately! On Death and Suicide 81
On the Eros of Species 95
The Benighted States of America? 108

PART THREE: PHILOSOPHICAL DIGRESSIONS

The Last of the Cartesians: On Enlightenment and its Discontents 125
Nietzsche's Cow: On Memory and Forgetting 142
Socrates Among the Cicadas: The Art of the Platonic Dialogue 159

Glossary 177
Index 185
About the Authors 190

Illustrations

1 *My Bed*, Tracey Emin, 1998. © 2014 Tracey Emin. All rights reserved, DACS, London / Artists Rights Society (ARS), New York. 10

2 *A Pair of Boots*, Vincent Van Gogh, 1887. The Baltimore Museum of Art: The Cone Collection, formed by Dr. Claribel Cone and Miss Etta Cone of Baltimore. 11

3 *Veiled Nun,* Guiseppe Croff, 1860. Photograph by Daderot, 2012. Creative Commons License. 36

4 *Temple of Poseidon from the East,* Wikimedia Commons, 2012. Creative Commons License. 41

5 Parthenon (Nashville), Mayur Phadtare, 2012. Creative Commons License. 42

6 *Fountain* (replica), Marcel Duchamp, 1950 (original 1917). © Succession Marcel Duchamp. ADAGP, Paris / Artists Rights Society (ARS), New York 2014. 46

7 *Electric Chair*, Andy Warhol, 1962. © 2014 The Andy Warhol Foundation for the Visual Arts, Inc. / Artists Rights Society (ARS), New York. 48

8 *Marilyn Monroe*, Andy Warhol, 1967. © 2014 The Andy Warhol Foundation for the Visual Arts, Inc. / Artists Rights Society (ARS), New York. 48

9 *Lichtdom* (Cathedral of Light), 1936. Bundesarchiv, Bild 183-1989-1109-030 / photograph: o.Ang. 53

10 "Socrates and Plato," frontispiece of *Prognostica Socratis Basilei*, Matthew Paris, 13th C. Oxford, Bodleian Library, ms. Ashmole 304, fol. 31v. 168

Introduction

The literary dialogue originated with Plato and Xenophon, who sought a form that would reproduce the dialectical give-and-take for which their teacher, Socrates, was both celebrated and condemned. Socrates himself believed that philosophy begins in doubt and proceeds through trial and error: that it is peripatetic in the mental as well as the physical sense. Philosophical wondering demands, in other words, a kind of literary wandering, an itinerant form that is exploratory, desultory, improvisational—more interested in the journey than the destination. As a genre, the dialogue has proven remarkably durable, generating not only Plato's extraordinary canon, but also some of the most memorable works of philosophy and literature in the West, from Boethius's *The Consolation of Philosophy*, Malebranche's *Dialogues on Metaphysics and Religion* and Fénelon's *Dialogues of the Dead* to Berkeley's *Three Dialogues Between Hylas and Philonous*, Landor's *Imaginary Conversations* and Wilde's "The Critic as Artist." The success of the dialogue has not, however, extended quite so confidently into the modern period, where with a few exceptions—one thinks of Santayana's *Dialogues in Limbo* or Murdoch's *Acastos:Two Platonic Dialogues*—it has mostly fallen out of fashion. In the hope of reviving this fading form, we have written ten dialogues on a range of topics relating to literature, art and culture. Our dialogues are, however, different from those named above because they are genuine exchanges: not monologues disguised as dialogues but a play of two distinct voices and two distinct minds engaged in cajoling, objecting, correcting and challenging but always questioning. In the process, we have attempted both to renew and reinvent the dialogue as a literary and philosophical exploration.

Our book is organized into three sections. Part One: "Art and Aesthetics" includes meditations on the aesthetics of banality ("Flaubert's Hat Trick"), the uses and abuses of recent literary

Acknowledgments

We would like to thank Claudia Egerer, Chair of English at Stockholm University, who first gave us the opportunity to bring *Platonic Occasions* before the public when she invited us to read a dialogue in the Higher Literary Seminars at Stockholm in 2012. We are grateful to Prof. Egerer not only for her gracious hospitality but also for her willingness to take a chance in the HLS on what is admittedly not the usual sort of academic fare. Our reception at Stockholm—at once generously collegial and probingly critical—was a model of the Platonic dialogue at its best. We wish especially to thank a number of the participants, which included Paul Schreiber, Thomas Lavelle, Maria Kuteeva, Stefan Helgesson, Bo Ekelund, Pieter Vermeulen, Irina Rasmussen Goloubeva and Charlotta Einarsson. We are also deeply indebted to Nils-Lennart Johannesson, a distinguished scholar of Linguistics and Medieval literature at Stockholm, who has been wonderfully supportive in shepherding our manuscript through the review-and-production process at Stockholm University Press. His many labors on our behalf—including translating computer software from Swedish into English—are much appreciated. We also want to thank Phillip Bandy, Michael Opest and Gaby Ruchames at the University of Wisconsin-Madison for their invaluable editorial assistance. Their keen eyes and quick minds lightened our lucubrations and prevented many embarrassing errors. Finally, Christiaan Marie Hendrickson in Madison and Janeen Barker in Canterbury have kept the home-fires burning as *Platonic Occasions* has gone from idea to reality. They are not merely our good spirits, but our better spirits—indeed all our *eudaimonia*—and it is to them that we dedicate this book.

PART ONE: ART AND AESTHETICS

criticism ("The Dysfunction of Criticism at the Present Time") and *mimesis* from the Greeks to the present ("The Grapes of Zeuxis"). Part Two: "Evil, Death, Love, Politics" examines evil from the Book of Genesis to Conrad and the Holocaust ("The Art of Darkness"), suicide and death from Shakespeare to Beckett ("Let's Hang Ourselves Immediately!"), the shrunken fortunes of *erōs* in modern life ("On the Eros of Species") and the troubling, poignant—and often hilarious—degradation of American culture ("The Benighted States of America?"). Finally, Part Three: "Philosophical Digressions" investigates Descartes and the Enlightenment tradition ("The Last of the Cartesians"), the philosophy of memory and forgetting ("Nietzsche's Cow") and the art of the Platonic dialogue ("Socrates Among the Cicadas").

Although we have entitled our collection *Platonic Occasions*, we are not ourselves Platonists. To the contrary, as students of Richard Rorty we trace our intellectual affiliations to a decidedly less idealist, less metaphysical tradition—to philosophers like Nietzsche, Heidegger, Wittgenstein and Derrida. Nevertheless, we are attracted to Plato and his canon for two reasons. First, our own dialogues focus on precisely the topics that most animated Plato's thinking and that he so memorably examined: love, death, good, evil, memory, art, representation and political governance. Second, we are attracted to the dialogue as a form, especially insofar as it registers the delicate movement and play of thought about a subject. While we have fundamental disagreements with Plato on a host of philosophical issues, we nevertheless believe that his writings are a good deal more open-ended, open-minded, indeed dialogical, than has generally been appreciated.

The dialogues in this volume were produced over several years as a series of e-mail exchanges. Some of the dialogues began when one of us posed a question to the other, with the ensuing conversation developing from that slender beginning. In other cases, we decided in advance to explore a particular subject, but never knew where our exchange would take us or to what conclusions it might lead. In all cases, we followed a simple but absolute rule: once an entry had been submitted it could not, under any circumstances, be revised. This meant that in our polemical back-and-forth if one of us got the better of the other—as occasionally happened—our triumphs and defeats were fully on display. Like a game of chess, there were no "take-backs," thereby guaranteeing the intellectual honesty and integrity of the dialogues. This commitment to preserving our exchanges as written keeps them, we hope, from feeling staged or formulaic—as is sometimes the case in Plato—and lends them a conversational immediacy.

All our dialogues address what are sometimes called the Big Questions: what is love, truth, art, beauty, evil and death? We are aware that such questions can never be answered, at least not in any final or definitive sense. But if we wish to experience fully what it means to be human—if we seek to live what Plato called the "examined life" (*Apology*, 38a)—then we must continue to ask these questions, not in the expectation of answering them but in the conviction that by striving to do so we will better comprehend who we are and what we might achieve. Martin Heidegger devoted much of his philosophy to what is called the *Seinsfrage*, a question that asks not simply "Why am I?" but more fundamentally "What does it mean to be?" And yet, if such a question admits of no answer, then what is the point of asking it? Here is what Richard Rorty says on this subject:

> I think Heidegger goes on and on about "the question of Being" without ever answering it because Being is a good example of something we have no criteria for answering questions about. It is a good example of something we have no handle on, no tools for manipulating—something which resists "the technical interpretation of thinking." The reason Heidegger talks about Being is not that he wants to direct our attention to an unfortunately neglected topic of inquiry, but that he wants to direct our attention to the difference between inquiry and poetry, between struggling for power and accepting contingency. He wants to suggest what a culture might be like in which poetry rather than philosophy-cum-science was the paradigmatic human activity. The question "What is Being?" is no more to be *answered correctly* than the question "What is a cherry blossom?" But the latter question is, nevertheless, one you might use to set the theme of a poetry competition. The former question is, so to speak, what the Greeks happened to come up with when they set the theme upon which the West has been a set of variations.

The dialogic experiment that Socrates inaugurated and that Plato immortalized understands that the questions most worth asking are precisely those that have no answers. These are questions that stand beyond the purview of the technocrat, the statistician or the actuary, questions that are best approached by accepting the contingencies of conversation and inquiry, the thrust and counter-thrust of minds caught in the act of thinking and attempting to feel their way around a problem, even if it means never arriving at a solution. As Socrates points out in *Apology*, the highest wisdom consists in recognizing the limits of one's own knowledge, which is to say, in acknowledging one's own ignorance. At the same time, it is worth remembering that Plato, whose ambition as a young man was to be a tragedian, employs the form of the dialogue to mix philosophy with literature. He creates characters, places them in dramatic situations and supplies them with witty and compelling dialogue. As everyone knows, Plato became the most celebrated critic of literature, the philosopher who infamously "banned the poets" from his "Republic." But—as we argue in our concluding dialogue—Plato's position on poetry in particular and the arts in general is a good deal more complicated than such a reading allows. Indeed, Plato's philosophy is a marriage of logic and rhetoric, one that weds the rigor of the thinker with the invention of the poet.

About halfway through Samuel Beckett's *Endgame*—a play very much concerned with the *Seinsfrage*—Clov asks that most existential of all questions: "What is there to keep me here?" Hamm replies, without hesitation, "The dialogue." The exchange is quintessentially Beckettian, at once deeply ironic and deeply earnest. We hope that our dialogues—which we have sought to make playfully serious and seriously playful—will suffice to keep readers here, keep them attentive and engaged. And if, along the way, what we have written diverts as well as instructs, we will be all the more grateful.

the words "Absolute Style" (Flaubert's own words in his letters to Louise Colet) are an abbreviation. That game has intrigued me for decades. And it makes one of my favorite novels also one of the funniest novels ever written. I think that in all the fuss made about Flaubert as a Realist, one forgets that he is also a humorist of the highest order, as boisterous as Rabelais, as witty as La Rochefoucauld, as darkly comical as Voltaire. What happens if we put on that imbecilic cap as a thinking cap, as Flaubert did for five years during the composition of *Madame Bovary*?

RB: Homer gives us epic *ekphrasis* with the shield of Achilles. Flaubert gives us bourgeois *ekphrasis* with the hat of Charles Bovary. And lest we miss the connection, the master of *le mot juste* drives home his classical allusion by calling the hat *une casquette*, variation on *casque* or "helmet." As you point out, the hat trick metamorphoses the base metal of everyday life into the precious gold of art. But it also—in wonderfully perverse and distressing ways—does the opposite: it suggests that Flaubert's precious metal may itself be fool's gold. And this is where the Homeric allusion again becomes important. For we must remember that it is Hephaestus who engages in the *poiēsis* or "making" of Achilles' shield. While Homer's poetic model is an Olympian deity, Flaubert's is a provincial hat-maker; while Homer is inspired by Heaven ("Sing, Athena, of the wrath of Achilles"), Flaubert's muse is a shopkeeper ("Sing, O Milliner, of the stupidity of Charles").

You of course know the letter of 16 January 1852 to Louise Colet in which Flaubert speaks of his desire to write a book "about nothing, dependent on nothing external, which would be held together by the internal strength of its style, just as the earth, suspended in the void, depends on nothing external for its support; a book which would have almost no subject." Charles's grotesque hat and the empty head it goes on is a symbol of this vacuity. In a sense, Flaubert's subject is his lack of a subject. In a sense, his art is about its own debasement into meaninglessness and insignificance.

John Updike once said that Andy Warhol's art has "the powerful effect of making nothing seem important." Of course, the "nothing" here includes Warhol's art. I would argue that this is

Flaubert's Hat Trick, Or The Pleasures of Banality

JS: I think it is Julian Barnes, in *Flaubert's Parrot*, who describes the French author as the "butcher of Romanticism and the inventor of Realism." I wonder if the latter accolade is fully justified by the well-known passage below that describes, in loving, hateful detail, the school-boy cap of Charles Bovary:

> It was one of those head-gears of composite order, in which we can find traces of the bearskin, shako, billycock hat, sealskin cap, and cotton night-cap; one of those poor things, in fine, whose dumb ugliness has depths of expression, like an imbecile's face. Oval, stiffened with whalebone, it began with three round knobs; then came in succession lozenges of velvet and rabbit-skin separated by a red band; after that a sort of bag that ended in a cardboard polygon covered with complicated braiding, from which hung, at the end of a long thin cord, small twisted gold threads in the manner of a tassel. The cap was new; its peak shone. (Translated by Marx-Aveling)

I am imagining the oratorical Flaubert, bellowing out those three sentences, five hours into his twelve-hour writing day, until the hideous hat of young Bovary begins to become, through the alchemy of style, a triumph of *le mot juste*, in other words, at once a simulacrum and an anticipation of the grand performance—the miraculous hat trick—that transforms a bored, petit-bourgeois farm girl, a voluptuously sentimental Emma, into *Madame Bovary*, a work of art. That hat is doubtless an example of both realism and symbolism, but its expressiveness—editorially insisted upon in the passage itself—is part of a new language game, for which

How to cite this book chapter:
Begam, R. and Soderholm, J. 2015. Flaubert's Hat Trick, Or The Pleasures of Banality. In: Begam, R. and Soderholm, J. *Platonic Occasions: Dialogues on Literature, Art and Culture*. Pp. 3–17. Stockholm: Stockholm University Press. DOI: http://dx.doi.org/10.16993/sup.baa.a.

precisely how Flaubert—living in the post-ideological aftermath of 1848—conceived of his own art. Charles Bovary's hollow headpiece is, in other words, the nineteenth-century equivalent of a can of Campbell's soup—presumably Vichyssoise rather than tomato—and Flaubert is painfully aware of the implications this has for his aesthetic project. His hat trick consists in creating a world "suspended in the void." But he remains uncertain whether his lapidary expression will be sufficient to supply the emptiness of his occasion. Bereft of deities, will he remain a Homer? Or will he become the literary equivalent of a provincial hat-maker, artfully gluing together felt and feathers?

JS: Given what "happens" in *Bouvard et Pécuchet*—the two clerks hovering over the void of their utter banality and uselessness—I think perhaps the hat trick becomes something almost Beckettian in its dire iterations. Is literary nihilism the result of the art of nothingness? Does Flaubert pass the hat to Beckett? I don't necessarily want to navigate away from our beloved *bovarysme*, but I wonder if you think this connection has any "substance" to it?

RB: Kant's genius was to have discovered the uselessness of art. Flaubert's was to have discovered the usefulness of banality. Taken together, they provide a text-book definition of *Zweckmässigkeit ohne Zweck*—of a purposeless purposiveness—and Beckett is their grateful heir.

But there is another antecedent to the art of uselessness and banality: William Wordsworth. You've spent a good deal of time meditating on Wordsworth's relation to Byron. What about his relation to Flaubert? The leech-gatherer is banal and his vocation largely useless, yet Flaubert's satire becomes Wordsworth's heroism. And what of the latter's Idiot Boy? How different from the imbecile Charles Bovary. And yet how similar.

JS: At first Byron spanks the hell out of the "Idiot Boy" in *English Bards and Scotch Reviewers*, but much later he writes "Unjust" in the margins of his own satire on Wordsworth. I think the so-called "democratization of subject matter" that is often attributed to Wordsworth goes back at least to Burns and his mouse and louse and perhaps also sends a taproot to Defoe's assiduous account of how Crusoe makes bread. When Wordsworth actually measures mud puddles in *Lyrical Ballads*, he anticipates later experiments in artistic banality, and no doubt the Idiot Boy somehow gives birth ("the child is the father of the man") to Charles Bovary. In both cases, a kind of expressive imbecility capers first as "Romanticism" and then as "Realism," although the actual experiments are, I think, far more interesting and entertaining than the "isms" that would purport to explain them.

But I am still left wondering what Byron meant by that belated judgment: "Unjust." Did he fail to imagine Wordsworth (in his early phase, at least) as a potentially comic poet? Is that failure somehow connected to an inability to see just how hilarious Flaubert is when he depicts Homais as the Bourgeois Satan? And yet, next to the shield of Achilles and Homer's epic grandeur, isn't there something truly miserable and depleted about making leech-gatherers into the stuff of poetry?

RB: Certainly Flaubert is participating in the democratization of subject matter, as Jacques Rancière has argued. But I wonder if his literary project isn't finally more radical than that. He is, after all, not simply valorizing the everyday, but insistently aestheticizing it. For him the kitschiest of objects—whether Charles's hat or Emma's heart—are not merely suitable subjects for the artist but the *only* subjects available to him. In a world where Bouvard and Pécuchet can imagine themselves as Diderot and d'Alembert, the artist's instrument is no longer a Homeric lute but a cracked kettle; and his melodies no longer make the stars—or the gods—weep, but set bears dancing. Translated to post-1848 France, Achilles' shield is a writing desk built for two idiots (one is not enough). Translated to 1960's America, Achilles' shield is a can of Campbell's soup reproduced a hundred times (it's simulacra all the way down).

When Flaubert famously proclaimed, with a nod to Louis XIV, "Madame Bovary c'est moi," he was being lethally comic and deadly earnest. A writer cannot escape his own time or place. It is not simply a rabbit that Flaubert has pulled out of Charles's hat. It is himself.

JS: It is the trickiest hat in town. For two decades students have asked me what "Madame Bovary c'est moi" means. Two things come to mind. Henry James referred to Flaubert's "puerile dread of the grocer" and Roland Barthes wrote that the "one thing we cannot avoid is being middle class." I think Flaubert's cracked kettle makes beautiful music, even in translation—the very thought of which must have made Flaubert's gorge rise—but that music, as you suggest, must necessarily be less grand than Homer's chanting, haunting, murderous dactylic hexameter. And yet why are we so mesmerized by Achilles slaying Trojan boys in a river? What is Homer's hat trick? To make murder beautiful? I think of Emma's death bed and the moment when, a few hours after she "ceased to exist," someone tilts up her head slightly and a stream of black blood pours like old motor oil from her mouth. Gorgeous sentences, disgusting details. It is not merely the only modernist language game in town, but really one of the oldest and most venerable games, or tricks. Life has always been essentially shabby. And art has always been essentially an attempt to turn it inside out, magically, so that the content vanishes and the purposeless purposiveness porpoises, breaking the surface, disporting as form, a shimmering arc.

RB: In 1861, five years after the appearance of *Madame Bovary*, Charles Baudelaire published *Les Fleurs du Mal*. The slender volume included a meaty little valentine called "Une Charogne." The poem begins conventionally enough with a young man asking his lady if she recalls a beautiful summer day they shared. But then it takes an unpredictable turn. In the remembered scene, the lovers come upon the grotesque remains of a rotting carcass, its legs thrust in the air "like a woman in heat." Here are four of the central stanzas, freely translated:

> The flies buzzed on the putrid belly,
> From which issued black battalions of larvae
> Flowing like a thick liquid
> Along a pile of living rags.
>
> The whole fell and rose like a wave,
> Or erupted into a sparkling foam;

One would have thought that the body,
Swollen by a vague breath, was living, multiplying.

This world emitted a strange music,
Like running water and wind,
Like the grain that a winnower, with a rhythmic motion,
Shakes and turns in his basket.

The forms erased themselves, became mere dream,
A rough sketch tentatively shaping itself,
On a forgotten canvas that the artist
Completes only in his memory.

If Homer kills boys in a river, Baudelaire murders love on a garden path. Of course, the carcass is itself a symbol. At one level, it provides a mordant commentary on the Lamartinian tradition of romance, a *memento mori* for all who would append "evermore" to the word "love." On another level, the carcass seems to reanimate itself, to take on a lubricious life of its own, insisting in darkly Sadean ways on *erōs*'s fascination with *thanatos*. Of course, what is important for our purposes is the relation between Flaubert's hat trick and what we might call Baudelaire's pet trick. The poet, like the novelist, is radically rewiring our aesthetic circuits, discovering beauty in the unlikeliest of places, demonstrating how art can transfigure rotting flesh into music, rhythm and dream. Just as Flaubert anticipates Warhol's soup cans, Baudelaire anticipates Robert Mapplethorpe's anal whip and Carolee Schneemann's vaginal scroll.

One might argue that these hat-and-pet tricks are profoundly Kantian. How better to demonstrate the artist's legerdemain than by showing how completely form has trumped content? Yet one could just as plausibly argue that these tricks are profoundly anti-Kantian. By corporealizing art, by rubbing our nose in its fleshy, shitty, mucous-laden materiality, artists like Baudelaire, Mapplethorpe and Schneemann destroy aesthetic disinterestedness. Life and art are no longer cordoned off from each other. The ontological divide that separated them is breached, and the everyday, the odious and the obnoxious tumble into the privileged space of Kantian aestheticism.

To what degree, I wonder, is the phenomenon I have been describing the result of an imperative to innovate? Does the endless drive to "rouse the faculties" (Blake), to "make it new" (Pound), to "negate tradition itself" (Adorno) lead to an art that is so perverse, trivialized and marginalized that it finally ceases to be art. In making art everything, did Flaubert and Baudelaire ultimately make it nothing?

JS: Indeed, and how far can art be (about) nothing and still be recognizable as art? The answer seems to be: one hell of a lot! You earlier avoided my reference to Beckett's contribution to the fecund imbecility we have been discussing. After all, our beloved tramps wore hats. Are Bouvard and Pécuchet (and Rosencrantz and Guildenstern before them) the forebears of Vladimir and Estragon? In negating both dramatic and novelistic traditions, did Beckett give us "sparkling foam" in his "spray of phenomena"? If you want to give this another pass for now, then why not hop into Tracey Emin's bed? Her *My Bed* (an installation of her actual bed strewn with underwear and condoms, the sheets stained by her unprecious bodily fluids) makes the cap of Charles Bovary look almost heroic by comparison. I think it's a short stroll from the loo (Duchamp's *Fountain*) to Emin's bed. Has "art" ever been so banal, so personal, so emptily symbolic, and so formally bankrupt? I have to imagine Turner doing about 4500 rpm in his grave, given that Emin was short-listed for the 1999 prize bearing his name. Now a British luminary of some repute, Emin has succeeded in making "art" out of the detritus of her cannily-disheveled, overexposed and depressive life.

If Emin's bed does not entice—and heaven knows why it should—then I suggest we walk around in Van Gogh's "Peasant Shoes" and recall Heidegger's phenomenological treatment of them. Apparently Van Gogh picked up the shoes in a flea market (the origin of the modern work of art?) but they were not sufficiently worn and beaten up for him so he walked around in them in the rain until they looked a bit more "peasanty," and then he painted their Heideggerean "truth" in all its miserable detail, thus taking us as far as possible from Plato's "Shoeness" in the direction of the "thingly" and "worldly" character of things and worlds.

Hephaestus did not cobble those shoes. Sing, O Cobbler, of the Truth of Peasants. We live in a time when the foul rags of the human heart have an odd vitality, when even mud puddles can rise into a wave. But I still think the exquisite corpse of art is strangely connected to Homer's performance, where fish rise to nibble on the blood streaming from dead Trojans as they float to immortality. And what do we make of how wrathful Achilles ends up in Hades, vaguely repenting his short, happy and murderous

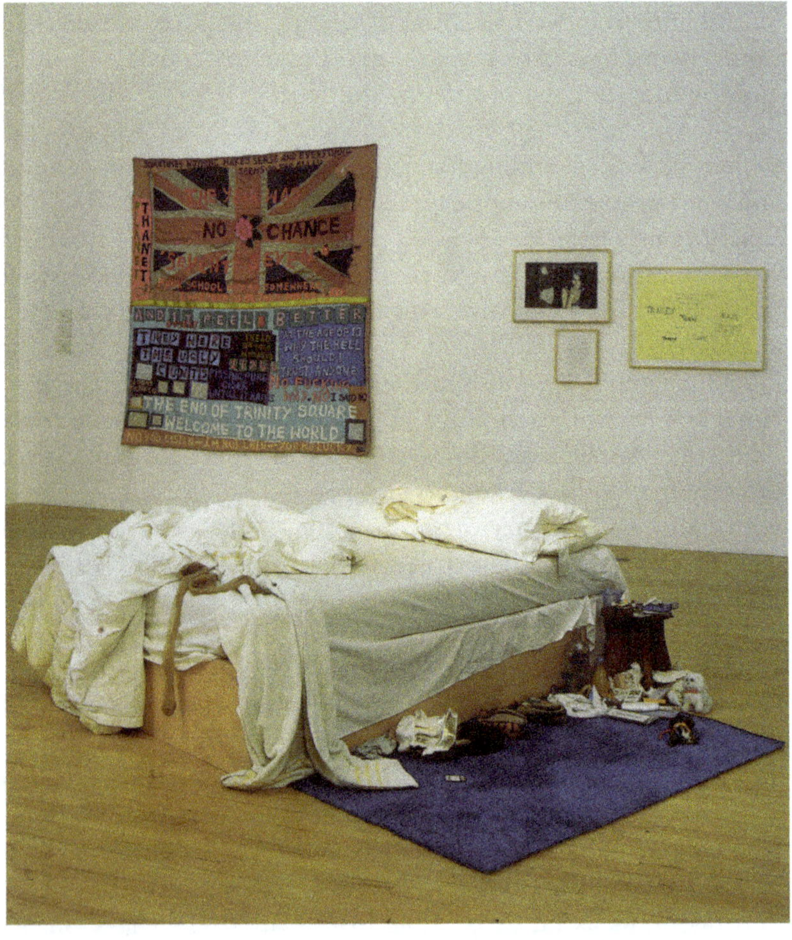

Figure 1: Tracey Emin, *My Bed*. (© 2014 Tracey Emin. All rights reserved.)

life, wishing he could return to life as Charles Bovary wearing Van Gogh's peasant shoes?

RB: Much is made of hats throughout Beckett's corpus. Usually they function as comic props for staging mind/body dualism as a series of music-hall gags. Lucky puts on his bowler to think, and Vladimir takes off his because it "irks" him, while Molloy secures a straw boater to his body with an elastic band. For Flaubert the hat is the symbol of an absent or evacuated mentality. For Beckett it is the symbol of a fugitive or contingent cognition. Both writers are post-Enlightenment figures, for whom the mind is in retreat. And yes, Vladimir and Estragon have many forebears, comedians and ironists all, from Laurel and Hardy, Bouvard and Pécuchet, Rosencrantz and Guildenstern to Quixote and Panza, not to mention Socrates and the Youth of Athens. Wherever mind dialogically examines itself, wherever it puts questions, invents answers, engages in repartee—there one finds Didi and Gogo.

Are Flaubert's and Beckett's banality the same as Tracey

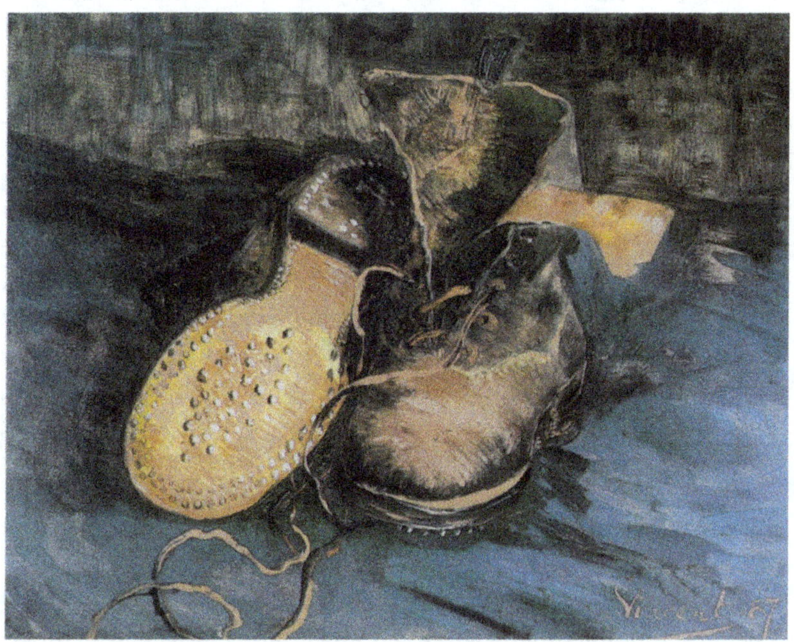

Figure 2: Vincent Van Gogh, *A Pair of Boots.* (The Baltimore Museum of Art).

Emin's? Ontologically speaking, yes. Critically speaking, no. Emin has produced a work of art—that is, a work whose function is aesthetic not practical. To be sure, one *could* sleep in her bed, but clearly a good-night's rest does not begin to describe its "purposive" structure. In the Kantian sense, its purposiveness is purposeless (it has no "real-world" function), which means that it belongs in a museum rather than in a bedroom; or, to speak more precisely, which means that it is a candidate for exhibition in a museum. A curator with any critical standards—which excludes the Saatchi Gallery and the Turner Prize committee—would reject Emin's work for the trash it is. In this regard, she has nothing in common with Flaubert and Beckett: they have produced great art, while she has merely engaged in narcissistic exhibitionism.

I think you are right to suggest that a continuum runs from Homer to Flaubert, Baudelaire, Van Gogh and Beckett. Artists have always worked with form and content. They must have something to say, and they must say it in a distinctive and compelling way. But much of the art we call modern is born out of a crisis of subject matter, a sense that we live in an age so frivolous, vulgar and insubstantial that the relation of form to content has become vexingly problematic. Flaubert and Baudelaire initiated a tradition in which the detritus of modern life emerges as a major preoccupation, the thematic axis of an art that is obliged to discover a form appropriate to its content. Warhol pushes this tradition to the brink of kitsch and then pulls back at the last minute, bracketing it with a kind of peek-a-boo irony. By contrast, Emin's art doesn't even know what kitsch is. Purposiveness has gone all slack and rumpled, and *poiēsis* has (like her bed) become so "unmade" that there's simply no "there" there.

The *ekphrasis* of Achilles' shield is a fit emblem for great art, which always opens up an alternative universe, one that is rich, complex, capacious. Emin's art is about as complex and capacious as a bag of dirty laundry. There is an inert literalness to it. She has the sensibility not of an artist but of a stock clerk.

JS: And that is precisely what separates Emin from Emma. For all her tedious and finally lethal sentimentality, Emma has, Flaubert tells us, "an artistic sensibility" that allows the author, however archly, to identify with her ("Madame Bovary c'est moi"). Emin might also say of her work—using a contemporary and blandly narcissistic idiom—"My bed, Myself" but this close alliance with one's work is a false intimacy and even less exciting and aesthetically compelling than getting into bed with yourself. The cap of Charles Bovary, to return to Flaubert's generative conceit, or fecundating *ekphrasis*, is not only the opposite of literalism—as we have suggested—but even beyond symbolism. It is the music of the future, all the more impressive because of its impoverished resources, like getting a Shostakovich symphony out of the xylophone of a rotting rib cage, or torturing a parrot until it sings like Mimi in *La Bohème*: modern art as a collection of cracked kettles implausibly wringing tears from the stars. The art of detritus and the detritus of art. I suppose we do need Homer's epic grandeur to "shield" us from modernity, postmodernity and the fact that art has become a hat trick, or a trick hat, that nearly makes us forget how much art has now "installed" itself as dirty laundry. Before we move back to another passage in *Madame Bovary*, I am naturally wondering how Eliot's *The Waste Land* fits into the picture we have been describing. All those broken images. All that impotence.

RB: Emin is, as you say, blandly narcissistic, but the problem is not narcissism per se as the cases of Proust and Joyce demonstrate, both of whom were colossally self-obsessed. If an artist takes himself as his subject, he needs to discover in that subject something more than his own identity—a broader significance that moves his art beyond literal self-presentation. The epiphany enabled Proust and Joyce to accomplish this. In their hands an ordinary object or event is transfigured, pushed into the realm of the transcendent. A cake dipped in tea becomes a communion wafer that shatters space and resurrects time; a girl on the beach becomes an aesthetic summons that forges the uncreated conscience of the race. Emin's bed, on the other hand, is a tired tautology. It functions according to the same logic as a blogger who documents what she ate for breakfast and all her visits to the bathroom. We cannot say the same of Charles's hat. Like Achilles' shield, it is a metaphor and a metonym for an entire culture and the art it produced. Similarly the fragmentation and impotence of *The Waste Land* acquire integrity and power, with Eliot re-imagining his personal suffering (he called the poem so much "rhythmic grumbling") as the experience of an epoch and its relation to tradition.

Mimi is an artist because she is able to sing about something other than herself. Emin sounds the same note over and over: Me, Me.

JS: We discuss narcissism and the "Me Me Tradition" in another dialogue in relation to Whitman's "Song of Myself," which stands to America rather in the same position as Virgil's *Aeneid* stands to Italy: as both national myth and founding epic. Whitman's experiment in combining a national epic with what Keats called "the egotistical sublime" produces some great poetry and some nauseating conceits, for example the line, "The scent of these arm-pits' aroma finer than prayer" from the opening of "Song of Myself." But those arm-pits are meant to be America's lovely stench, not merely Whitman's, an expansiveness that puts him leagues beyond Emin's fetid bed. That aroma, as distinctive in its own way as tea-soaked madeleine cakes for little Marcel, evokes an entire world, or perhaps a body-politic.

I'd like to return to Madame Bovary for a moment and another "cap" of sorts. This one is the cake constructed for the wedding of Emma and Charles:

> A confectioner of Yvetot had been entrusted with the tarts and sweets. As he had only just set up on the place, he had taken a lot of trouble, and at dessert he himself brought in a set dish that evoked loud cries of wonderment. To begin with, at its base there was a square of blue cardboard, representing a temple with porticoes, colonnades, and stucco statuettes all round, and in the niches constellations of gilt paper stars; then on the second stage was a dungeon of Savoy cake, surrounded by many fortifications in candied angelica, almonds, raisins, and quarters of oranges; and finally, on the upper platform a green field with rocks set in lakes of jam, nutshell boats, and a small Cupid balancing himself in a chocolate swing whose two uprights ended in real roses for balls at the top.

I like to think of that outrageous wedding cake as an echo of the description with which we began this dialogue. Like Charles's hideous hat, the wedding cake is an assemblage of disparate parts—"heterogeneous materials by violence (egg)yoked together"—that suggests a talent for ransacking various cultures and mythologies in order to make them purely decorative. In other words, out of the kitchen, kitsch: a sweet confection where Greek porticoes are made of cardboard. It is just the kind of wedding cake—elaborate, sentimental and voluptuous—that Emma would have loved to create (did she give the confectioner instructions?). The wedding cake as a well-wrought, if not overwrought, urn: an object of wonderment and a joy forever.

Flaubert presents us with a series of failed or fake artists in *Madame Bovary*, people struggling to be "artistic" but ending up as hacks, charlatans and mere confectioners of beauty. Emma herself is such a failed artist, struggling to make her house into a work of art (a French Martha Stewart) and, failing in that, struggling to make her life into a work of romantic fiction, the kind of fiction she read in the convent as a girl. The most hilarious and obscene example of the pretentious but failed artist is Binet, Yonville's tax collector, who bends over his would-be lapidary lathe to turn out hundreds of napkin rings (pure purposelessness). We are on our way to Warhol's soup cans, except without the saving irony—and without Flaubert's contempt for such mass productions, the verbal equivalent of which he catalogues so assiduously, comically and pungently in his *Dictionnaire des idées reçues*, which he also called an "encyclopedia of human imbecility," the same imbecility that one sees in the cap of Charles, whose "dumb ugliness has depths of expression." Obsessed with *le mot juste*, Flaubert pours scorn on all those who haven't his genius for that alchemy by which "patterns of provincial life" (the novel's subtitle) become ornate, precise and beautiful sentences. Flaubert is also a confectioner of words, but the wedding cake *he* builds is a minor work of art, not a laughable piece of kitsch. He performs this hat trick over and over in *Madame Bovary* so that we can mark the distance between the artist and the hack, a distinction lost in a world where filthy beds and hoaxing artists take away prizes, like Homais receiving, in the last sentence of the novel, "the cross of the Legion of Honor."

RB: If the hat is a synecdoche for Charles's head, the cake is a synecdoche for Emma's bed, her imagined romantic and erotic life, which combines temple, dungeon and fortification with sugary illusion. And as you observe, the cake is both an art object in its own right (a Tower of Babel built of *mots justes*) and a symbol of what art becomes in bourgeois culture: a form of domestic ornamentation. Of course, the novel itself is the form par excellence of bourgeois and domestic culture, a fact that Flaubert both understands and exploits.

In *Theory of the Novel*, Georg Lukács remarks, "Art always says 'And yet!' to life. The creation of forms is the most profound confirmation of the existence of a dissonance." Art needs the idiotic and jumbled mess that is the object-universe of bourgeois culture, all those disparate and conflicting styles that make Charles's hat and Emma's cake into a potpourri of kitschy excess. Homais' receiving the Legion of Honor at the end of *Madame Bovary* is typically read as Flaubert's mordant comment on the inevitable triumph of mediocrity and mendacity in nineteenth-century France. But I wonder if Flaubert's relation to Homais isn't more complicated than that. After all, Flaubert's Absolute Style has transformed even a despicable pharmacist into a well-wrought object, art's "And yet!"—its "O mais!"—to life. I think something of the same transformation, though admittedly in a far more sympathetic vein, takes place with both Charles and Emma. And it has everything to do with such grotesque creations as the hat and the cake.

Somewhere Walter Benjamin speaks of the trashy, mass-produced objects that furnished the comfortable home of his Berlin childhood. While he later recognized that many of these objects were pure kitsch, he nevertheless retained a profound affection for them because of the memories they carried. One of the most startling aspects of Flaubert's genius is his ability to ironize—almost to the point of obliteration—all the shoddy bric-a-brac of bourgeois culture, while at the same time reproducing it with what can only be described as a lover's attention to detail. He hangs on the hat and the cake as Romeo hangs on Juliet's lips. So too with Flaubert's characters. If Emma is ultimately redeemed by her passion—her poignant and rather desperate belief that there is more to life than the banality of provincial existence—Charles is ultimately redeemed by loving Emma for her passion—which is to say, by loving Emma for hating everything he represents. One can imagine nothing further from the narcissism of Tracey Emin.

Here, in the Steegmuller translation, is the final scene of the novel:

> The next day Charles sat down on the bench in the arbor. Rays of light came through the trellis, grape leaves traced their shadow on the gravel, the jasmine was fragrant under the blue sky, beetles buzzed about the flowering lilies. A vaporous flood of love-memories swelled in his sorrowing heart, and he was overcome with emotion, like an adolescent.
>
> At seven o'clock little Berthe, who hadn't seen him all afternoon, came to call him to dinner.
>
> She found him with his head leaning back against the wall, his eyes closed, his mouth open; and there was a long lock of black hair in his hands.
>
> "Papa! Come along!" she said.
>
> She thought he was playing and gave him a little push. He fell to the ground. He was dead.

What is the most profound love? The one in which the lover becomes the beloved. Cathy is Heathcliff, and in his final hour Charles is Emma. To his credit, Flaubert never succumbs to sentimentalism. Charles's flood of love is "vaporous," and he is overcome with emotion like "an adolescent." Can anything be more clichéd than dying for love, as Charles does? And yet (O mais!) can anything be less like Charles than dying for love? How far has he traveled beyond himself—beyond his own clichés—to become someone else's cliché? In a sense, Flaubert reverses the terms proposed by Benjamin. An object that initially struck us as pure kitsch, has begun to acquire value, substance, meaning. Flaubert has himself redeemed his Idiot Boy. Should we now, à la Byron, write in our own margins "Unjust"?

JS: Unjust and *juste* simultaneously. Great art puts us right there.

The Dysfunction of Criticism at the Present Time

JS: Here is an episode, a memory, from my first year as an Assistant Professor at the University of Wisconsin-Milwaukee. My colleague, Ihab Hassan, was giving a talk about contemporary theory, radical skepticism and the excesses of the hermeneutics of suspicion. Already weaning myself from that school of thought and thinking about a New Aestheticism, I was keen to hear his lecture. Hassan's office was next to mine, and I often chatted with the great man and "inventor" of Postmodernism. He seemed relieved that I wasn't another dreary post-Althusserian, neo-Marxist Foucauldian who, as Wordsworth put it, "murders to dissect" works of literature so that the helpless creatures will disclose their nefarious and deleterious ideological subtexts, etc., etc.

Hassan decorated his superb lecture with some of his favorite moments of poetry, if only to show, as he said, that "language can be good" (not a tissue of hateful lies subjugating some Subaltern or Other). During the question and answer period at the end, a feminist graduate student launched her hand and said, "I was insulted by how you brought out the dancing girls every so often." By this she referred to Hassan's favorite bits of poetry, his personal miscellany of lyric goodness that suggested his ideologically-suspect "love of literature." Dancing girls. I was appalled. In that assault on Hassan's good will towards literature, I first detected what I would like to call "the dysfunction of criticism at the present time." My echoing Matthew Arnold is, of course, canny. And I wonder what you make of the fact that for

---

How to cite this book chapter:
Begam, R. and Soderholm, J. 2015. The Dysfunction of Criticism at the Present Time. In: Begam, R. and Soderholm, J. *Platonic Occasions: Dialogues on Literature, Art and Culture*. Pp. 18–34. Stockholm: Stockholm University Press. DOI: http://dx.doi.org/10.16993/sup.baa.b.

most of our professional lives, the following judgment of Arnold would be considered anathema:

> But criticism, real criticism, is essentially the exercise of this very quality; it obeys an instinct prompting it to try to know the best that is known and thought in the world, irrespective of practice, politics, and everything of the kind; and to value knowledge and thought as they approach this best, without the intrusion of any other considerations whatever.

RB: The feminist deconstructionist and the Arnoldian humanist are the obverse and reverse of the same coin. She believes in the artlessness of truth, he in the truthfulness of art. Both are idealists seeking a language that escapes Nietzschean *Allzumenschlichkeit* and Rortyean contingency. She wants to get rid of the dancing girls, and he wants the "best" that is known and thought. But "best" for what? How we define exemplarity depends on context and function. There is no outside to the language game, no master discourse that transcends discourse. I would have responded to the graduate student with a simple question: "How can we know the dancing girl from the dance?"

More generally, I'm skeptical that all those literary-theoretical -isms ruined criticism. For me, the wind that blew out of the Continent in the 1960s and into the musty halls of the Anglo-American academy had a mostly enlivening effect. So far from rendering criticism dysfunctional, the French and German schools—structuralism, post-structuralism, hermeneutics, reception theory, Marxism, etc.—gave new purpose and direction to the reading of literature. The problem was not Barthes, Foucault and Derrida, or Benjamin, Adorno and Iser, but a tedious and tendentious group of American academics who turned the dancing girls of the Continent into a parade of politically-freighted clichés.

JS: I take the "best" to refer to the value of being raised among beautiful exempla, including the best and most beautiful literature. To that extent I am a Platonist, I suppose, in believing that we have, as Lionel Trilling put it, a "moral obligation to be intelligent." I also have an obligation to preserve and uphold what I can loosely yet confidently call the content of a properly liberal arts education before that undertaking became nearly synonymous with a politicized, canon-busting "democratization" of literary studies. Let us forge ahead by being radical: rooted in a liberal imagination that enjoys the broadest possible set of connections between literature and culture without being a belligerent advocate for either a pristine formalism or a fatuous materialism. I am not plumping for a master discourse. I would make a case for English departments where one can observe a huge range of options for students, from the unashamed, vulgar Marxist to the unashamed, refined Formalist. They all have their version of dancing girls. But no one is rude or close-minded enough to call them that. Am I mistaken or has the latter creature nearly disappeared from the groves of Academe? And are we breeding students who really cannot tell the difference in quality between F. Scott Fitzgerald and James Joyce?

RB: You evoke Arnold and Plato and speak of the Beautiful, the True and the Good as though they were out for a joy-ride on a bicycle built-for-three. But these estimable qualities have little or nothing in common. Put them on a tandem and they will end up wrecked in a ditch or hedgerow. You of course know the concentration camp argument. Germany was one of the most highly educated and intellectually refined countries on earth in 1940. *Ruhrgebiet* factory workers listened to Furtwängler conduct Beethoven with rapt attention (I've seen the photos). And yet the program in the camps was murder by day and Mozart by night. All that beautiful *Bildung* did nothing to ensure right conduct. To the contrary, it produced one of the most catastrophic moral failures in human history. Returning to Hassan and the graduate student, we should remember that it is the grim feminist and the prim Victorian who strive to connect art and ethics. I share Kant's view that criticism, real criticism, only begins when we have drawn category distinctions that separate Reason, Morality and Beauty.

Having said that, I agree that literary studies in the academy have become dysfunctional, and one of the principal reasons for the current mess is ideologically-motivated reading. But I don't think we should "radically" forge ahead by returning to Trilling's idea of the "liberal imagination." What you propose is

Trilling's update of Arnold with a dash of pluralism thrown in: the Deconstructionist Lion lies down with the Formalist Lamb. I would suggest something more radical: a return to a rigorously hermeneutic tradition in which the critic seeks to identify and calibrate Meaning and Significance—*Sinn* and *Bedeutung*—according to such criteria as text, intention, production and reception. Jerome McGann has attempted this kind of highly layered and deeply textured reading with results that to my eye are extremely promising.

JS: I am not arguing for a literal or strict connection between art and ethics. I am suggesting that aesthetics—except in the rare case of the Nazis and a few other maniacs vended to us by history—always already dovetails with an ethical stance. Marxists and Feminists tend to ossify or literalize what is actually the most subtle and supple of sinews: that which makes many novelists (and their readers) incapable of cruelty and of being what Rorty calls "monsters of incuriosity." Proust could satirize his world but would not hurt a fly. Artists never murder. Beethoven was hard work as a man, but he never would or could kill anyone, and his *Ninth Symphony* has lifted millions more hearts than it has hardened or furnished with easy escapism. The aesthetic, properly conceived, quickens tenderness and curiosity. That's why even the acerbic Jane Austen is, finally, a gentle Jane, a forgiving ironist, a satirist and a shaper of kindred souls.

RB: William Burroughs shot and killed his wife during a drunken game of "William Tell." Norman Mailer stabbed his second wife with a penknife (how wonderfully symbolic!) and nearly did her in. Verlaine shot Rimbaud in a jealous rage and but for his bad aim there would be no *Illuminations*. Villon was in and out of jail his entire life and ended up murdering a certain Sermaise in a wine-sodden altercation. And Christopher Marlowe—a man who vied in reputation with Shakespeare—was killed after assaulting a companion over a drinking bill. One could of course expand upon this list, and if we include the number of writers who fought in wars—where no doubt the usual unspeakable atrocities were committed—the roll call of death and dishonor expands. Artists never murder? Gentle Janes all? I think not. Creative souls often mind neither their aesthetic nor moral manners.

JS: What can I say? I don't think your list of murdering artists can match up to the much longer list of artists who spent all their time trying to both gentle and complicate our souls by setting us off on what Verlaine called—rather beautifully—our "adventures among masterpieces." Your impressive handful of artist-thugs is just that. And not one writer on your list can hold a candle to Homer, Virgil, Dante, Shakespeare, Milton, Wordsworth, Tennyson, Hardy, Eliot, Joyce, Yeats and Beckett (I could go on and on). By the way, recent scholarship suggests that Marlowe ran afoul of Walsingham and his murder was actually a political assassination.

But let us swerve from artists and return to criticism for a few more dysfunctional moments. I don't think there are many Jerry McGanns left in the American academy. For every subtle and responsible critic (who can still write), I suspect there are three academic lemmings lining up to jump off the cliffs of their craggy hermeneutics of suspicion. Did you know, for example, that public school children in the U.K. are currently being fed the idea that Heathcliff represents the underclass or proletariat who returns to overthrow his oppressively-bourgeois masters? A Marxist reading of *Wuthering Heights*? Why not? If gentle Jane Austen can be tortured (most famously by Eve Sedgwick) into saying that her novels are about female masturbation (or its repression), then I suppose any dysfunction is possible.

RB: I was responding to your rather startling assertion that "artists never murder." My argument is that artists are a mixed lot—some good, some bad, some dreadful—and that there's no connection between the quality of their morals and the quality of their art. Ezra Pound, Louis-Ferdinand Céline and Wyndham Lewis were raving anti-Semites and enthusiastic supporters of Hitler and Mussolini. When Pound learned of the Nazi slaughter of Jews in Russia he responded with a line that scans beautifully: "Fresh meat on the Russian steppes." And yet Pound, Céline and Lewis are three of the greatest artists of the twentieth century.

You say that "aesthetics always already dovetails with an ethical stance." I say where is the evidence?

As for criticism, it is indeed in a sorry state. But we have arrived at that state precisely because our reading of literature continues to be informed by a residual Arnoldianism. The Marxist and the Feminist both believe, along with Arnold, that art should morally instruct and improve. They simply disagree about what is instructive and what is improving. As I suggested earlier, hermeneutics offers an antidote to such moralizing by insisting on the distinction between *Sinn* and *Bedeutung*, a text's Meaning and a text's Significance. That distinction enables us to see that a great deal of current criticism falls into what philosophers call a "category error." Literary scholars often think that they're interpreting a text—attempting to understand its Meaning (what the author intended)—when in fact all they are doing is discussing its Significance for contemporary culture. Of course for the professoriate, contemporary culture means university culture, and university culture means a predictable set of political commitments.

JS: In stepping [over] slain meat, metrical feet create poetry, which is—as Pound says—"news that stays news." Poetry makes [the] new/s fresh flesh. Pound's line is not murder; neither is it murderously cruel. On the contrary, it intensifies—and prolongs—through the trick of style the horror of the Nazi slaughter, not unlike how Homer's dactyls intensify the taste of spilt Trojan blood. That's my sensibility, at least.

As for the professoriate, I have not much to add to your own comments. They are debasing Arnold. If art does instruct and delight, then the sensitive, intelligent critic must attend to how it does those wonderful things. What nettles me most is the assumption that art is hawking ideological biases and making us more miserable once we discover the designs it has on us. Irvin Ehrenpreis once said that criticism should be 90% information, 10% interpretation. Now we have 10% interpretation and 90% cultural significance. Scholarship is mostly dead. And academics paradoxically increase their irrelevance the more they bray about their importance as "public intellectuals" who can teach nineteen-year olds how to read *Pride and Prejudice* as a vagina monologue.

RB: But your own wonderfully perverse reading of Pound betrays the same kind of interpretive excess you condemn in the Marxists and Feminists. Given what we know of Pound's biography, it is clear that he was not registering his horror at the slaughter of Russian Jews, but celebrating what he saw as a fascist triumph. Why is it objectionable to transform *Pride and Prejudice* into a vagina monologue or *Wuthering Heights* into a Marxist revenge tragedy, but not objectionable to rewrite Pound's Jew-hating remark?

So far you have avoided responding to my comments on the distinction between Meaning and Significance. Both E. D. Hirsch and Jerome McGann—in their very different ways—believe that authorial intention is something critics should attend to. What is your view? My sense is that you want to have your hermeneutic cake and eat it. You like frisky, risky readings when you do them. But you hate them in Terry Eagleton or Eve Sedgwick.

JS: My frisky readings are risky only in the sense that they are sometimes original. By "original" I mean nothing more or less than that they attend in precise ways to the origins of the work of art 1) in its author's creative consciousness, 2) in its various cultural and historical contexts and 3) in my own evolving sensibility. This triad forms a kind of circuit within which my literary criticism sparks itself. I take on board your remark about my misreading of Pound's anti-Semitism. But, for me, the final effect of his "Fresh meat on the Russian steppes" is less to affirm or endorse the poet's baleful biases than to shine a torch on them in such a way that we can augur at once his hateful views and their stylization in poetic discourse. That Pound's unpleasant prejudices can be pleasantly scanned (in every sense) makes them important, memorable markers of the intersection of the lethal and the lyrical, the Unjust and *le mot juste*.

I don't like critics who are tactless in their friskiness. They grope the work of art in order to find what most obsesses them. The work of art becomes merely a platform or stage for the critic's hermeneutical floor-show of fantasy. One example of felonious friskiness should make my point.

I once heard a lecture by Susan McClary on Beethoven's *Ninth Symphony*. A feminist musicologist, she was on the verge of winning the coveted MacArthur Fellowship that nourishes promising geniuses. She argued in her lecture (subsequently published) that in Beethoven's *Ninth* the "point of recapitulation in the first movement of the *Ninth* is one of the most horrifying moments in music, as the carefully prepared cadenza is frustrated, damming up energy which finally explodes in the throttling murderous rage of a rapist incapable of attaining release." That sentence rightly provoked a huge debate called "Beethoven and the rape controversy." McClary considerably softened her tumescent reading in a later publication, but the mischief—and damage—had been done. I am hardly alone in seeing the excesses of McClary's "friskiness." Did she commit some sort of category error? At the very least, I would say that her "creative misreading" licentiously strayed from what one might call "tactful friskiness"—oxymoron cheerfully celebrated. But how much of criticism in the last forty years has been dominated by tactless, insensitive, overweeningly-suspicious habits of mind?

RB: Yes, the hermeneutics of suspicion has dominated much criticism of the last forty years and, yes, McClary's infamous Beethoven remark is an embarrassment. But I find many of her writings smart and incisive. I think Charles Rosen gives the most balanced account of her scholarship in "The New Musicology," where he observes that the impact of gender studies on musicology has been "uneven," producing work that ranges "from the enlightening to the loony." He commends McClary for her "racy, vigorous, and consistently entertaining style" and for her fine ear ("she hears what takes place musically with unusual sensitivity"), but he recognizes that her criticism often relies as much on showmanship as scholarship: "When she inflates her ideas, her purpose seems to be not so much to dazzle, or to attract attention, as to shock." At what point does shock become schlock and tactful friskiness "licentiously stray" into "overweening suspicion"?

As for your reading of Pound, Hans-Georg Gadamer would approve insofar as it fuses "originary" horizons—that is, insofar as it combines textual production, textual history and textual reception. In that sense, your approach is fully hermeneutic. But when you say the "final effect" of Pound's line is not to affirm the poet's biases but to expose them, the crucial phrase in your formulation is "*for me*." This is where one moves from *Sinn* to *Bedeutung*—from what the author intended to how it is "significant" for a particular reader. An anti-Semite apprehends "fresh meat" from one angle, a non-anti-Semite from another, and perspective may be determined as much by the author's meaning as by the reader's beliefs and desires. But—here things get complicated—there's another dimension at work here, which you have rightly insisted on. By visually and aurally heightening the image, Pound not only draws attention to what he describes, but also breaks down habitual patterns of perception. The effect is not to *align* morality with art, as Arnold would argue, but *potentially* to make available a new mode of seeing. And new modes of seeing *may* enable the reader to understand the world with a little more complexity, a little less reductiveness. Then again, as the example of the fabulously well-read Pound illustrates, it may not. In any event, it is in this area of indeterminacy that the relation of art to ethics becomes interesting.

One wonders if Plato and Aristotle, who wrote so influentially on this subject, are of any help here?

JS: Although Hermes was a Greek lad, I don't think the Greeks were all that hermeneutically sophisticated. For Plato, art and artists could remain in the *polis* if they were thoroughly ideal and idealizing. For Aristotle, the question is not whether art is good for the *polis* or its citizenry, but whether the work of art is harmoniously—and therefore powerfully—constructed; that is, if it is formally as "realized" as it can be. Even *katharsis* is subsidiary to that concern for—shall we say—the compelling "formality" of art. So if Plato would chuck out parts of Homer's *Iliad* where the hero is not acting like an ideal hero, Aristotle would sniff unpleasantly at a poorly-wrought tragedy if its plot were not, strictly speaking, in order. I'm not sure how those two ways of seeing art (the extrinsic and the intrinsic, the Platonic and the Aristotelian) graft onto our present discussion of Pound, Arnold, art, ethics and Beethoven, but perhaps they do if we could "only connect" them.

I do think "new modes of seeing" are precisely where the aesthetic kisses the moral. In one of his essays, George Steiner says, rather formally, that "whatever complicates consciousness is a high moral act." Beethoven's symphony does that, but McClary's work does not. In fact, her bellicose reductiveness is not only ridiculous: it is immoral. It is the horrifying aesthetic formality of "fresh meat on the Russian steppes" that makes the line at once so haunting, disgusting, beautiful and repellent. Only in news that stays news—because it is formally-stirring—can contradictory meanings and energies be held together in a way that makes us *see* (perceive, witness, comprehend, fathom, judge) more fully. Any critic who does not attend to—and take joy in—that miracle of dialectical tension should be banished from any Republic of Criticism. I admire truly *literary* criticism where the interplay between the work of art and the critic's hermeneutical friskiness is a peculiar form of intimacy where you *may* want to shoot the message and yet invite the messenger inside for a long evening of mutual dalliance. In the case of Hassan's miscellany of lyrical moments, his "dancing girls," one would be a fool to scare off *that* harem. It would be like killing a mockingbird.

RB: How we understand the function of criticism depends on how we understand the function of literature. Insofar as critics have considered literature socially significant, they have understandably worried about its moral effect. Plato and Aristotle provide two of the earliest accounts of that effect: the mimetic and therapeutic. It is well known that Plato regarded art as a poor imitation of ultimate reality, of the transcendent realm of the *eidos*. What is less well known is that Plato, like Oscar Wilde, also believed that reality—social and historical reality—imitates art. People are moved by an action in Homer, a character in Sophocles, a caress in Sappho, and they *imitate* what they have read, seen or heard. But since for Plato poets are more rhetoricians than philosophers, more interested in arousing emotions than promoting the Good, they are unreliable moral legislators and therefore dangerous to the body politic. Hence their banishment from the Republic.

Aristotle agrees that art has moral consequences, but he takes an approach radically different from Plato's. The affective dimension of art, the fact that it stimulates and manipulates the emotions, is for Aristotle not its weakness but its strength. Art functions like a good therapy session: it does not repress our darker impulses but isolates and exposes them, so that they may then be purged through *katharsis*. For Plato, seeing Oedipus sleep with his mother and kill his father promotes incest and patricide, but for Aristotle what happens in the Theatre of Dionysos stays in the Theatre of Dionysos. The audience is cleansed of its baser desires precisely by vicariously experiencing them.

Of course, both Plato and Aristotle are right. Young Weimarians dressed in blue jackets and yellow vests and put bullets through their heads in imitation of Werther. But plenty of other young Germans got all that *Weltschmerz*—not to mention *Weltschmaltz*—out of their system by reading Goethe's both wonderfully and ridiculously overwrought book.

So where does this leave us? I'm less convinced than you that "new modes of seeing" necessarily improve our ethical sensibility, and I reject Steiner's claim that "whatever complicates consciousness is a high moral act." But in a sense we are dancing around—speaking of dancing girls—the fundamental question of this dialogue, so I shall now ask it. Does literature—or, if you prefer, art—have a moral obligation? And if not, then what function does it serve?

JS: Only a tiny handful of Werther suicides are on the books and Goethe said he wrote the novel to "get it out of [his] system," so Aristotle mostly wins that battle. As for banishing the poets from his Utopia—well, it's a bit of a tangle. Plato's argument is fairly specific and, finally, perhaps deftly ironic, as some scholars have suggested in books with titles such as *Plato's Defense of Poetry* (Julius Elias). Nietzsche first suggested that line of defense when he claimed that in order properly to judge (and outmatch) the poets, Plato had to become a poet, almost despite himself. Hence, the literary and rhetorically-skillful dimensions to some of the dialogues, most notably *Phaedrus* and *Symposium*. Plato's Socrates discusses getting rid of *parts* of Homer's *Iliad* but certainly not the whole thing. He also discusses getting rid of certain pastries because they are too rich and fattening. One begins to suspect that Plato is not entirely serious about his astringent moral judgments regarding what gets thrown out of his Republic, that his stance might be shot through with ironic posturing. Plato's own use of myth (*poiēsis* as myth-making), moreover, indicates that philosophy must sometimes rely on similes, allegories and other literary devices to make a bridge to those who resist straightforward didactic philosophizing. A dialectic is, after all—as we keep demonstrating—a fundamentally literary enterprise, a language game partly sustained by its rhetorical performances or, to speak metaphorically, its dancing girls.

As for art's "moral function," I think that oscillates happily between Plato's and Aristotle's insights about art that you adumbrated. Throw in Horace and Longinus. I don't really feel the need to take sides, but I do think that in superior works of art the extrinsic and the intrinsic approaches are both fully justified. If I had to choose, I probably would plump for Aristotle because I think that most art functions less to urge than to purge.

As for the critics, I wish only that they would approach literature with a little more respect for the ways in which it represents a triumph of Mind far superior to anything critics do. I am helplessly reminded of one of my favorite exchanges in *Waiting for Godot* when Vladimir and Estragon decide to while away the time by insulting each other. The triumphant insult says it all:

> ESTRAGON: That's the idea, let's abuse each other.
> *They turn, move apart, turn again and face each other.*
> VLADIMIR: Moron!
> ESTRAGON: Vermin!
> VLADIMIR: Abortion!
> ESTRAGON: Morpion!
> VLADIMIR: Sewer-rat!
> ESTRAGON: Curate!
> VLADIMIR: Cretin!
> ESTRAGON: (*with finality*). Crritic!
> VLADIMIR: Oh!
> *He wilts, vanquished, and turns away.*

RB: Yes, Plato is more complicated than his banishment of the poets from the Republic would suggest. Yes, not every teenage reader of *Werther* lodged a bullet in his head. And yes, critics are a dreary lot and should show more respect for the artists they criticize. But (again) we cannot address the function of criticism until we address the function of art. You want to split the difference between Platonic models of conduct and Aristotelian mechanisms of therapy. We might also throw in the Kantian approach, which involves what we have been calling "new modes of seeing" (Viktor Shklovsky's *ostranenie* or defamiliarization). All three of these approaches assume a social function, although Kant is careful to take the "moral" out of the equation.

Might we say that Plato, Aristotle and Kant treat art, especially literary art, as providing us with what Wittgenstein described as "forms of life"? "To imagine a language," Wittgenstein says in *Philosophical Investigations* "means to imagine a form of life," a way of being in the world, of making choices and acting upon them. Literature provides us with models of living, mechanisms of feeling, modes of perceiving, and these in turn guide and shape the decisions we make and the life we choose. It does not, however, assure that those decisions and choices will be moral any more than reading the Bible or the *Nichomachean Ethics* inspires one to help little old ladies across the street.

But if we agree that literature provides us with "forms of life," the question remains what is the function of criticism? Is it to explicate what authors intended when they imagined a particular form of life? Or is it something else, something more? And if so, where do we draw the line between what the critic half perceives and half creates?

JS: I take your point, at long last, about the dubiousness of saddling art with a moral mission. As Nabokov tirelessly reminds his readers, "*Lolita* has no moral in tow." My argument or claim all along is that great art somehow gentles our condition, Nazi concert-goers notwithstanding. On the whole, I think the "forms of life" you mention conduce to make people more interesting, entertaining, soulful, complicated, and *possibly* less damaging to others if their moral imaginations are quickened by reading stories about people who are brutal to others precisely because they do not use their imaginations. The most decorous example of that quickening could be the lesson Jane Austen's Emma learns at Box Hill when she insults Miss Bates, much to the dismay of the assembled picnickers, particularly Mr. Knightley, who sternly chastises Emma for her lack of feeling towards the poor, garrulous spinster. But to be alive to *that* lesson of charitable good manners—what Austen calls "those elegant decorums"—one must not be starving (Shaw: "Get your money first, then your morals") or crippled psychologically. I don't know if that quickening amounts to the "social function" of art.

I honor critics—Tony Tanner in the case of Austen—who seem to pay close attention to what's on the printed page at the same time they make startling connections textually, intertextually, culturally, biographically, etc., and yet without making the literary text into an allegory of a single, supervising theory. Great literature will always overwhelm any theory meant to explicate it. And sometimes the critic's biases really do pervert the text, as in the [in]famous case of Chinua Achebe's reading of Conrad's *Heart of Darkness*. So, I think the purpose of criticism is to illumine and partly join in the dance of seven veils, both showing how those veils are put on and how they may be peeled off, one by one, to help reveal more and more unfamiliar beauty. If finding/making so much beauty somehow makes us into less perfidious, cruel and selfish human beings, so much the better.

RB: "Quickening" puts the matter nicely. Literature is, as the ancients never tire of telling us, a form of instruction. It educates not only the mind but also the senses. We might call it, as Flaubert did, a form of "sentimental education." But—here I gather we now agree—that education cannot and should not guarantee moral rectitude.

Achebe's "An Image of Africa: Racism in Conrad's *Heart of Darkness*" provides a text-book example of the hermeneutic issue I have been stressing insofar as it blurs the distinction between what the author intended and how those intentions strike a contemporary. Achebe acknowledges Conrad's historical situation ("It was certainly not his fault that he lived his life at a time when the reputation of the black man was at a particularly low level"), but Achebe nevertheless pillories the Polish writer for depicting Africans as "savages," given the fact that the Congolese art of the period was highly sophisticated. Indeed the masks produced by the Fang people of the Congo region later inspired Picasso and Matisse to revolutionize modern art. But it is here that historical precision is important. Maurice Vlaminck first circulated the African masks among Western artists in 1905. Conrad was in the Congo in 1889. Roughly fifteen years mark the difference between one "image" of Africa and another, and that historical difference is crucial to any fair assessment of Conrad's novella. Achebe's essay commits three fundamental errors. It fails to separate the moral from the aesthetic; it fails to separate meaning from significance; and it fails to historicize. As a polemic the essay is engaged and engaging. As serious literary criticism it is mostly useless.

JS: Achebe fails to understand the complex meaning of *Heart of Darkness* and that's *why* he condemns it. Properly absorbed, *Heart of Darkness* is at once a stirring critique of Belgian rapacity and a contemporary document in racism. The novella also contains materials for a dozen, perfectly responsible interpretations, my favorite being Michael Levenson's superb essay, "The Value of Facts in *Heart of Darkness*." Unlike Achebe, Levenson responds to intention, text, context, history, philosophy, psychology and aesthetics in order to evolve a sensitive and complicated understanding of the way Conrad shows how value-laden "facts" really are, more so as we journey into the dark hearts of both Kurtz and colonialism.

To see the novella *only* as a racist text is to misread the text and its author's intentions. To me, art is the opposite of propaganda, and we are back to the question of Pound's anti-Semitism. Achebe wrongly imagines that *Heart of Darkness* is propaganda for European superiority and in doing so he ignores how well the novella scans as anti-European and as a story about the disintegration of a mind in the jungle—for starters. It is the task of the critic, as T. S. Eliot observed, "to be very, very intelligent." The responsible critic must, at the very least, strive for something resembling "disinterested contemplation" rather than allowing his or her interpretations to be tainted by disfiguring—and dysfunctional—biases (Beethoven's music is a rapist, Conrad is a racist, etc.). Just as art is not propaganda, so criticism is not obsession, nor theory mere fantasy.

Piloting myself between the Scylla of Concrete Detail and the Charybdis of Abstruser Musings, I quickly tire of the "brilliancies of theorizing" unless the theories are truly brilliant. Even Stephen Dedalus, after "all in all," does not believe his own theory. Better to sacrifice a few speculations than to watch all one's works and days vanish in the devouring vortex.

RB: I think we have stumbled toward agreement. Literature is neither form nor content, neither the dancer nor the dance. It is both at once, acting in concert, and occurring in a specific time and place. Serious critics plot their course of explication along an array of vectors, including authorial intention, historical context, cultural situation, origins of production and horizons of reception. And they do all of this while remembering that literature is always an aesthetic as well as a semantic phenomenon—that it not only communicates meaning but also engages, indeed delights, the senses.

The crisis in literary studies at the university is not simply a matter of political correctness. It is also—I would say principally—a crisis in disciplinarity. Professional literary critics often have little idea of why they do what they do, beyond some vague sense of what will yield dividends in the scholarly marketplace. The result is the dysfunction of criticism at the present time.

As for theory, it has a significant role to play in revitalizing criticism, if only we had a theory worthy of the name. On my reading, Stephen Dedalus and James Joyce both believe in the efficacy of theory. Of course, Stephen plays many roles, one of which is Jesus, and he therefore speaks many languages, including the language of parable and allegory. His "theory" of *Hamlet* is really a theory of *Ulysses*, which is to say a theory of modernism. What he disowns is the literal application of the theory. Its allegorical application—the point where theory meets art—tells another story. But to understand that story, we must possess sufficient knowledge and skill to integrate the text that is *Ulysses* with the history that produced it and the theory that inevitably informs our reading of it. It is only then that the body will sway to music and the dancer will begin to dance.

JS: And that's precisely when and where the detached, intelligent and intuitive reader of literature understands that Hassan's dancing girls are not merely decorative, far less ideologically-suspect. They are forms of beauty—and forms of life—that unite our imaginations and judgment in such a way that we become capable of beautifully *literary* criticism.

The Grapes of Zeuxis: Representation in the Arts

RB: Erich Auerbach and Walter Benjamin were both born to assimilated Jewish families in Berlin in 1892. Both later studied literature at the German university, and after Hitler's rise to power both fled the country of their birth, Auerbach traveling to Istanbul and Benjamin to Paris. More importantly, during their exiles they both produced what are arguably the twentieth century's two most influential studies of representation in the arts: Auerbach's magisterial *Mimesis*, penned in Turkey and completed in 1946, and Benjamin's brilliantly provocative "The Work of Art in the Age of Mechanical Reproduction," written in three versions between 1935 and 1939. Are the connections between these critical essays merely coincidental, or do they run deeper, converging in significant ways on the aesthetic, the social and the political? Is it an accident that these works were produced by refugees from National Socialism and the mass propaganda it generated? Finally, are we justified in discovering parallels between *mimesis* in literature from Homer to Woolf and *mimesis* in photography and cinema? Indeed, might we extend the arguments of Auerbach and Benjamin to the simulacral culture of our own time—to mechanical reproduction as it exists on YouTube, Facebook and Twitter? Is the scar of Odysseus just another version of Paul Muni's and Al Pacino's *Scarface*, which itself anticipates the on-line fascination with Tina Fey's facial scar?

JS: Nietzsche observes that the ancient Greeks "were superficial out of profundity." I suppose, by contrast, that we moderns are, as you witheringly intimate, "profoundly super*facial*." The

How to cite this book chapter:
Begam, R. and Soderholm, J. 2015. The Grapes of Zeuxis: Representation in the Arts. In: Begam, R. and Soderholm, J. *Platonic Occasions: Dialogues on Literature, Art and Culture*. Pp. 35–55. Stockholm: Stockholm University Press. DOI: http://dx.doi.org/10.16993/sup.baa.c. License: CC-BY-NC-ND.

simulacra that variously divert us are three or four removes from Plato's Forms. But this is not the tack I want to take.

Our old friend and enemy, Jacques Lacan, thought the story about the two painters—Zeuxis and Parrhasius—showed that animals are compelled by appearances but human beings, with their oversized frontal lobes, are in love with secrets—the hidden, the mysterious, the veiled. It is one thing to fool the birds into descending with their bird-brains to peck fecklessly at painted grapes. It is quite another to paint a curtain so enticingly that one tries to pull it off the painting to reveal what it hides. Who was it—Frank Kermode?—who said that all great literature is based on a secret, on what the representation does *not* re-present, but makes at once pruriently and intellectually absent?

Yet another veiled illusion/allusion. I wonder if my reply to you, in the spirit of your inquiry, could take the form of reproduction/representation. And so my "re-ply" is my favorite piece of sculpture, which I recently admired in the Corcoran Gallery in Washington D.C. The marble veil and the face were of course chiseled simultaneously by the crafty artist. I am achingly intrigued by that simultaneity.

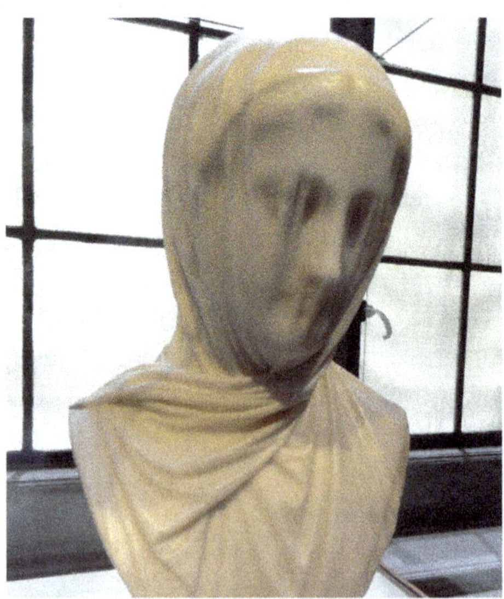

Figure 3: Guiseppe Croff, *Veiled Nun.*

RB: Lacan has forgotten the Greeks—or confused them with animals. Auerbach argues that there are two styles of representation in the West: the Hellenic and the Hebraic. The former depends on an aesthetic of externality, on beautiful surfaces and seductive appearances, while the latter depends on an aesthetic of internality or transcendence, on depths that must be plumbed and heights that must be scaled. In Hellenic art, meaning and expression are effortlessly integrated—the one inhering in the other—but in Hebrew Scripture the reader labors to find the meaning below the expression, struggles to close the interpretive distance between surface and depth. Benjamin's program is different but related. For him the contrast is between the aura of traditional art and the mechanical reproduction of photography and cinema. With the advent of a xerographic technology, the ability of art to enchant or mystify—its auratic function—is destroyed. Before mechanical reproduction, the work of art is characterized by its *uniqueness* (there is only one *Mona Lisa*) and by its *distance* from the viewer (we must travel to view Leonardo's masterpiece). But once we can endlessly and effortlessly duplicate the *Mona Lisa*, the painting's uniqueness and distance are destroyed, with the result that we lose the quasi-cultic function of art.

Guiseppe Croff's sculpture, *Veiled Nun* (1860), coyly illustrates Auerbach's and Benjamin's notions of art. We must pierce the veil, penetrate the surface, see into the depths of the sculpture in order to apprehend it properly. The veil stands for a kind of interpretive resistance that prevents us from moving beyond appearance to essence. In chapter two of *The Genesis of Secrecy*, Kermode writes "If we want to think about narratives that mean more and other than they seem to say" then we should consider the "parable." Croff's sculpture presents a parable that is a paradox: the veil renders the secret visible, draws our eyes to the unseen, detains us in the fold (as did your re-ply) that deliciously joins surface and depth.

JS: I think part of what so intrigues me about *Veiled Nun* is the lack of resistance that allows us to see at once the face beneath the veil and the veil itself. It is a paradox or a kind of phenomenological conundrum. Add to the mystery the fact that a face, too, can be a veil, especially a nun's face, which may serve both to reveal and veil a woman's interiority, her spirituality and her sexuality. But, to me, there is something hermeneutically suggestive about that sculpture and its transparent secret. Pondering both gaps in clothing (slit skirts that reveal, suddenly, a flash of flesh) and gaps in texts (moments where the reader is invited to author meaning), Roland Barthes wrote: "Is not there the most erotic place—there, where the garment leaves gaps?" One also recalls the lasciviously gap-toothed Wife of Bath and her radically "heterotextual" "Preface," which—busy with quotations from authoritative texts—both reveals and hides (adds a layer of skin, or a skein) to the Wife's intention to find Husband Six on her way to Canterbury. No veiled nun, the Wife, but one can still get lost in her "folded" sexuality/textuality.

I wonder which is the more "advanced hermeneutics"—the Hellenic or the Hebraic? Does not Auerbach plump for the former? Does not *Veiled Nun* somehow combine or fuse the two kinds of interpretation, or perhaps even short-circuit them precisely because its distinctive, magical aura turns depth into surface, surface into depth, in a single moment, at first glance and at last gaze?

RB: For Auerbach, the Greek text is transparent, the Jewish text opaque. Does he prefer Olympian cloudlessness or Mosaic abstraction? The epistemology of the surface or the hermeneutics of depth? Critics tend to incline to the latter, though one suspects that Auerbach's categories are more dialectical than oppositional. Certainly the great essays in *Mimesis*—"Odysseus' Scar," "The World in Pantagruel's Mouth," "The Weary Prince," "The Brown Stocking"—organize themselves around an interplay of surface and depth, and it is that interplay that *Veiled Nun* so beautifully illustrates. Insofar as we see through the veil, it is transparent, but insofar as we see the veil itself, it is opaque. It is a kind of membrane (one thinks of Derrida's "Tympan") that mediates between, while joining together, outside and inside. Or if you prefer, it is a version of Kermode's "parable" (from the Greek *parabolē*), which carries suggestions of "comparison," "illustration," "analogy." "Like" but not "is," the parable occupies that ambiguous space "between," the Barthesian gap of interpretive play.

In Book XIX of *The Odyssey*, Euryclea recognizes Odysseus by his scar—she "reads" the surface—and yet the scar itself has "deeper" significance. It is at once the sign of his rite of passage to manhood (symbolically wounded in the thigh, he nevertheless kills the boar) and also a portent of his future success (he will vanquish the suitors and reclaim his throne). The scar looks backward and forward in time. It is confined to a fold of skin, but beneath it lies a complex, temporal archaeology, a narrative chain of interlocking analepses and prolepses.

Similarly Croff's veil—a curtain of air and a sheet of marble—seamlessly flutters in its polysemy. At one level, the veil is simply itself, not a sign but a surface, a garment worn by a nun, the literal expression of her "having taken the veil." And yet, as a moment's reflection shows, this cannot be the case. Nuns wear wimples not veils and, whatever their head-covering, they never show their hair. Might the veil of this well-coiffured woman be a sign for something else? Notice that as the fabric falls to the woman's neck, it tightly winds around her throat, enclosing, grasping, strangling. Is Croff offering his commentary on the fate of the young woman, drawing an analogy between the veil and the noose? Indeed, pushing matters further, might we say that this is not a veil at all, but a shroud? Notice her lifeless eyes, the forward-drooping head, the preternaturally peaceful expression of her face. Perhaps Croff is suggesting that having taken her vows, she is now dead to the world. But let us slip deeper into the folds of this hermeneutic unravelling. Might the delicate membrane that covers her face be meant to remind us of another membrane—one that will forever remain intact, unpenetrated, inviolate? Croff has sculpted both the death of love (she is buried alive) and the love of death (the essence of Christianity). It is at once a parable itself and a parable about parables (all those veiled allusions).

But here I think it is worth pausing to remind ourselves of a simple fact. What you and I have been talking about is not *Veiled Nun*, which is a life-sized bust housed in the Corcoran Gallery, but a two-dimensional image, approximately 2½ inches by 3 inches, which exists in hyperspace. My question: have we been discussing Croff's sculpture at all? And if not, what is the relation between the mechanically produced image you imported into this dialogue and that sensuously arresting piece of marble in Washington, D.C.?

JS: The bad news: the "pixilated" *Veiled Nun* has no aura at all once she is torn from her gallery setting and wanting her third dimension. The good news: I can look at her whenever I fancy, which is often. Indeed, I can now stroll through most of the major art galleries and museums in the world whilst sitting at home and staring at my computer. I cannot think that is necessarily a degrading, degraded activity, despite my not being radiated by or bathed in the sensuous, ritual aura of the original work of art.

Even a mechanical reproduction of *Veiled Nun* gives me a certain *frisson.* I imagine Croff, chisel in hand, working in the least diaphanous of materials (marble) and banging out both a lovely face and a lovelier veil *with the same stroke* of the small hammer. The illusion produced is one of the most enchanting and engrossing I have ever come across. It trumps every *trompe l'oeil* I know—and I've known quite a few.

RB: Your pragmatic response (mechanical reproduction has its advantages and disadvantages) makes perfectly good sense, but I suspect that philosophers like Benjamin and Heidegger would claim that it ignores a larger aesthetic question. For them, the work of art fundamentally changes—is transformed in its essential being—when it becomes a simulacrum. For Benjamin, those changes are potentially liberating: the function of art shifts from "ritual" to "politics," with all that promises (from Benjamin's perspective) for social progress. For Heidegger, those changes are profoundly destructive: the work of art in losing its origin loses its ability to open itself to truth. In both cases, mechanical reproduction fundamentally alters the ontological status of the work of art.

To speak in Heideggerian terms, when the veil is no longer palpable or present, when the Greek temple loses its cultic function, it ceases to be a Greek temple. Veil-less, it is unable to draw us into the "unveiledness" of *alētheia.* The work of art becomes a piece of archaeology, a ruin of its former self, a simulacrum of what it was.

JS: It's not the ontology of *Veiled Nun* that appeals to me, or the lack thereof because she is missing one dimension. Even as a reproduction, the piece's astonishing craftsmanship and splendid illusion comes through every time. Do I prefer visiting her—my sacred, marbled mistress—in Washington, D.C.? Yes, of course, but her "presence" on my computer screen is not hugely diminished because she is merely an image. As for Heidegger, I don't think his ontology has much to do with certain aesthetic responses that are both supple and subtle, as you have so ably demonstrated above in your writing about a work of art you have seen on your computer screen. In this particular case (I am a case-by-case man) *Veiled Nun* really does it for me "in person" or in reproduction.

Now, the Parthenon rebuilt in concrete in Centennial Park in Nashville, Tennessee—that, my friend, is another case altogether. Behold this aura-less travesty of a mockery of a sham.

RB: Given our discussion of *Veiled Nun*, I would have thought Heidegger's "truth-as-unveiling" would flutter your imagination a

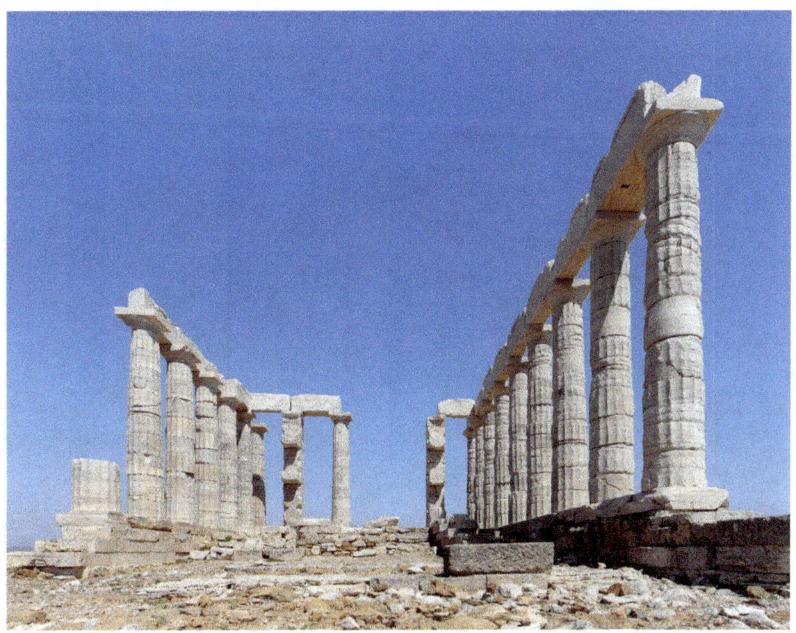

Figure 4: *Temple of Poseidon.*

bit more. If not, let me pass on to the Nashville Parthenon and ask a simple question: assuming that it is a structurally exact reproduction of the original, would your opinion of it be different if it had been executed in marble rather than concrete? In other words, taking it as a perfect replica (marble and all), wouldn't your local version of the Temple of Athena be just as good as the one on the Acropolis? Indeed, wouldn't it be even better, because you would have it, so to speak, in your backyard?

JS: Materials matter. There is something obscene and kitschy about a concrete Parthenon. And the damned thing is already decaying after just over one-hundred years. I called your attention to the Nashville Parthenon precisely because it is so devoid of its ritualistic aura in its Dixie setting. Having said that, imagine all those bus-loads of school-kids who will never see the original on the Acropolis. Perhaps a few of them will be enlivened by Greek art and culture because of their tramping through the concrete Parthenon (they don't care that it's not marble). It is also not reduced to ruins (yet), but a perfect scale model that gives you

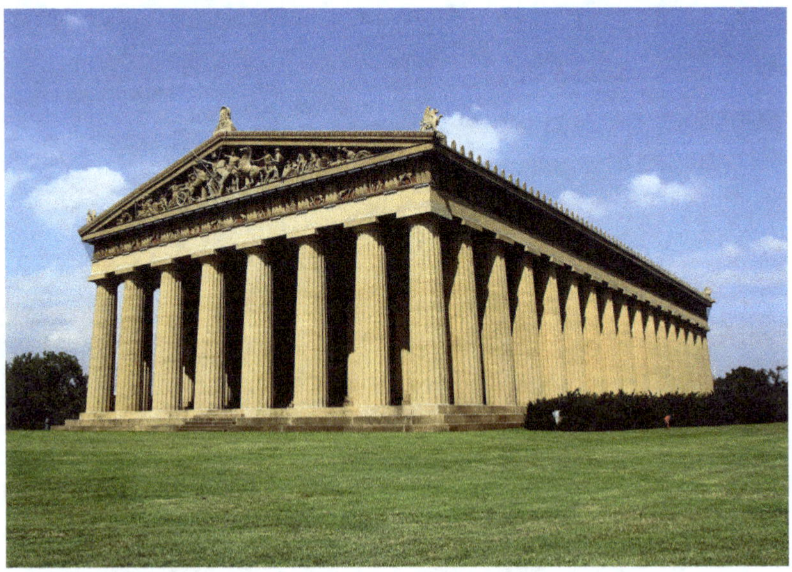

Figure 5: Nashville Parthenon. (Mayur Phadtare, 2012. Creative Commons License)

a far better sense of the lovely symmetry and graceful proportions of the original. What's astonishing is that the good citizens of Nashville would ever have constructed their "Parthenon" in the first place—and over a century ago, when the South was, one imagines, far less culturally-astute than it is now.

RB: And the answer to my question is ... ?

JS: I prefer certain reproductions to others, case by case. I have no purchase on the precious "aura" of most works of art anyway, so why pretend otherwise?

RB: Yes, case by case. And the case before us is the Nashville Parthenon. Would you object to it if were an *exact* replica, if it were identical in form and material to the original?

JS: If reading T. S. Eliot has taught me anything, it's that modern life—even one hundred years ago, but probably even 2000 years ago—is miserably demythologized and de-ritualized for most people crawling from womb to tomb. That goes for *any* viewing of any Parthenon, the one in Athens or the one in Nashville. To amend Heidegger: "we are too late for ritual, too early for Being." Even if you put the handsomely, "romantically" ruined Parthenon, marbly piece by piece, in Nashville, I would not be "aura-struck" by it. Let us remember our Wittgenstein: To imagine [the language] of ritual is to imagine "a form of life." And I am necessarily utterly divorced from any form of life that would make the Parthenon glow or radiate its magic. By the way, the same divorce holds for my appreciation of Canterbury Cathedral, which I can see from my desk at this very moment. Have I finally answered your question, Dr. Benjamin?

RB: Pragmatist that I am, I too have no use for the cultic function of art, whether it involves radiating auras *à la* Benjamin or "worlding worlds" *à la* Heidegger—though it is worth remembering that Benjamin himself was of Brecht's party and therefore celebrated the triumph of an aura-less "political" art over an aura-packed "traditional" art. I pressed you on the question of the

Nashville Parthenon because it seems to me that at a minimum art, as opposed to craft, does require a fully individualized source or point of origin. If I make a copy of the *Mona Lisa*, I haven't produced a work of art but a forgery. Of course, in our contemporary "down-load" culture, there is no such thing as origin or originality or copy: it's simulacra all the way down.

But there are real-world consequences to the aesthetic of the simulacrum. Our relation to the work of art is profoundly altered. It is not simply that the "work" of art loses its "workly" status, the sense that it is the product of an act of labor, which required time, thought, energy, design, talent, craftsmanship and perhaps even a little genius. The reception of the work of art is also profoundly altered. When Ruskin communed with the Italian masters, he didn't peruse a book of reproductions, surf the Internet or take a virtual tour of the Doge's Palace. He literally trod the stones of Venice. And rather than "capture" on his iPhone the paintings and architecture he saw, he painstakingly entered detailed sketches of these wonders into his portfolio. His relation to the art he described was fundamentally—indeed ontologically—different from our relation to art in the Age of Mechanical Reproduction.

JS: Like Adam, I am tempted to accept and fatally munch on your apple from the Tree of the Knowledge of Authenticity and Reproduction, especially since in my well-wrought, diurnal rounds, I pass by Walter Pater's "wave after wave of stone" called Canterbury Cathedral and "get" almost nothing out of it, as I mentioned a few exchanges ago. My benumbed students cannot tell me—I perversely ask them every two weeks—how many towers the Cathedral has in total. The Cathedral is, like Latin, a dead language, hardly aesthetically compelling or, indeed, perceptible, for most of the dead pilgrims that obligingly, during sweet or cruel April, sojourn here to wander through it. The very possibility of ritual has degenerated into deadening routine, which is also largely the point of *The Waste Land*. So perhaps I am even more hideously grim than you are on this point because, just strolling to work, I witness tourists by the thousands treating The Real Thing as a Reproduction even as they pretend to adore it.

And yet I have to wonder (and make you wonder) how far Art has *ever* been sensuously entangled with ritual and myth. For every ancient Athenian who made the pilgrimage up the steps to the Acropolis to moon over *Athena Parthenos*, there must have been thousands who did not want the Parthenon to happen, who just walked dully along, looking for a good ouzo fix and scratching their innocent Greek arses on the nearest olive tree.

RB: Your rounds may be diurnal but I don't for a moment believe that a slumber has sealed your aesthetic spirit. Indeed you and I have, of a summer's day, lingered on the vast lawn that joins The King's School with the Cathedral, transported by that gravity-defying, heaven-ascending behemoth, delighting in its every line, lineament and volume. There may not be a God, but anyone who has really *seen* the Cathedral will understand why men once believed in Him.

Has art always been the purview of the privileged few? Certainly aesthetic souls have been complaining about philistine indifference since antiquity, as Petronius's *Satyricon* so memorably illustrates. Nevertheless, I think Benjamin is correct when he argues that with the advent of mechanical reproduction "the total function of art is revolutionized." This revolution has extended itself most profoundly and pervasively in our time as a form of simulacral culture. When everything becomes digitalized, virtualized, plugged in, it is no surprise that your students no longer apprehend the Cathedral, let alone the civilization that produced it.

Of course, there's nothing new or interesting in whinging over the fact that we've all gone digital. After all, I'm sitting at my own computer right now, as you may be at yours. What does interest me—and perhaps is worth thinking about—is how modernism may have contributed to the general degradation of aesthetic perception in our own time. I'm rather fond of Marcel Duchamp's famous 1917 "ready-made," *Fountain*. By signing it R. Mutt (with its pun on the German *Armut* or "poverty"), he reminds us that a poor man's fountain (not to mention art) will be decidedly less elegant than a rich man's. Duchamp has added just enough to his ready-made—and its deconstruction of Kantian anti-utilitarianism—to make it a witty commentary on the materiality and function of art.

Having said that, I was nevertheless amused to discover the image shown below, which the "curators" of Google Images scrupulously inform us is a reproduction *not* of Duchamp's 1917 "original" but of a 1950 "replica." No doubt there is a substantial difference in monetary value between the two objects. But is there *any* difference in aesthetic value? Indeed, does it make sense to distinguish between originals and replicas when talking about *Fountain*? For that matter, would it be possible to make a "forgery" of Duchamp's sculpture? Presumably it would be a "replica" masquerading as an "original," though of course the whole point behind a ready-made is there *is* no original. Which leads me to a question: Once it's simulacra all the way down, is there any way back up—back up to those towers your students can no longer see?

JS: Did you know that beer-swollen tourists regularly pee—or try to pee—in *Fountain*? Well, they do, according to museum employees. That it is impossible to pee—or try to pee—in or on

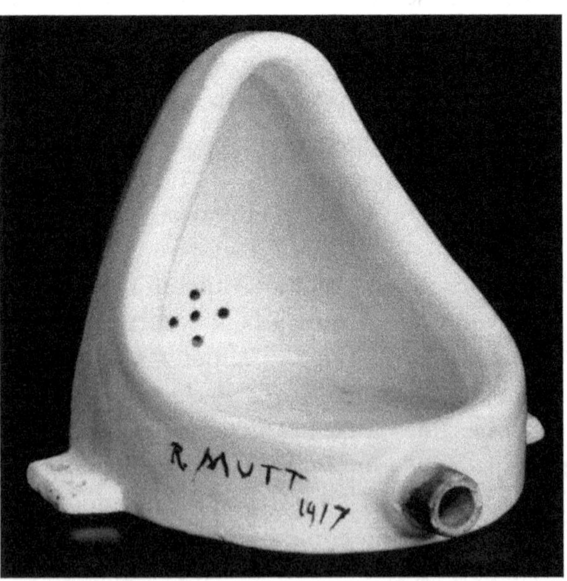

Figure 6: Marcel Duchamp, *Fountain* (replica). (© 2014 Succession Marcel Duchamp)

Veiled Nun must say *something* about what has happened to "Art" in the modern world. For *hoi polloi*, the "original" is so mimetically compelling that one might as well empty one's bladder in it. Or is Art so tedious and jejune that one can treat it as the chance to void one's wasteland of Miller Lite? Are we Paterians the judge of *anything* once the idea of judgment, both artistically and critically, has become shit—or once the veil has been torn and shredded?

RB: Zeuxis' birds peck and Duchamp's tourists pee. In both cases, viewers respond to what we might call the mimetic imperative, except in the case of *Fountain* the work of art is not an imitation but the thing itself. Or is it? Arthur Danto would say once Duchamp's ready-made enters the museum it has become art.

JS: I categorically reject Danto's formulation and the whole "institutional" definition of art. That's how Tracey Emin was anointed—by the pretentious Saatchi.

RB: One may disagree with Arthur Danto's "The Artworld" but one must give reasons. You begin to sound like Testadura, Danto's version of the philistine in the museum.

I might point out that the principal artist Danto is defending in his classic 1964 essay is not Tracey Emin, or one of the other Saatchi artists, but Andy Warhol. Here is Warhol's 1962 *Electric Chair*: mechanical reproduction meets mechanical destruction. Care to comment?

JS: I shan't defend Warhol. I cannot imagine one of his works that makes me think or feel profoundly. "Pop art" is, for me, an oxymoron that appeals only to lovers of mass culture, camouflaged as chic art critics. You are clearly not among them. Art, as I understand it, dies miserably in that electric chair. The electricity is a kind of didacticism, all the more shocking for being slyly but finally insufficiently ironic. If we want to ponder *Veiled Nun*'s evil twin/s, how about Warhol's "Marilyn" series?

RB: I think Warhol is one of the major artists of the second half of the twentieth century. He is to the America of the 1960s

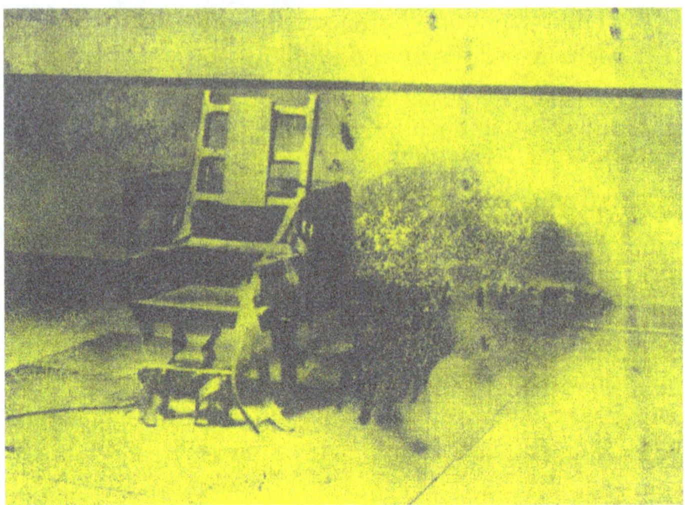

Figure 7: Andy Warhol, *Electric Chair.* (© 2014 The Andy Warhol Foundation for the Visual Arts)

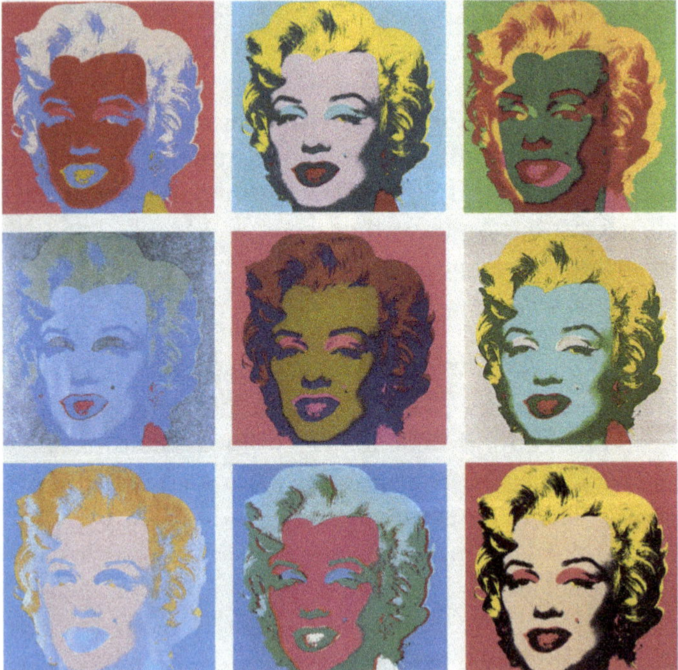

Figure 8: Andy Warhol, *Marilyn Monroe.* (© 2014 The Andy Warhol Foundation for the Visual Arts)

and 70s what Flaubert was to France of the 1848 Revolution, the Second Republic and the Second Empire. Both men constructed their art out of the popular culture of their time. In the case of Flaubert, it was sentimental novels, political journalism and the "democratization" of knowledge, as represented by the nineteenth century's reimagining of *L'Encyclopédie*. In the case of Warhol, the bill of particulars is familiar—from Hollywood to Madison Avenue to Celebrity Culture. Part of Warhol's brilliance consists in his having been the first artist (and this in the face Clement Greenberg's strictures on modernism) not merely to abandon abstract expressionism but to glory in the naïve imagery of mechanical reproduction. Of course, Warhol ironically distances himself from that reproduction—indeed introduces into it a commentary that savagely skewers the culture of xerography, even as it documents the ways in which celebrity has replaced aura.

Veiled Nun is lovely and provocative. But a hundred years from now everyone will know who Andy Warhol is, while today virtually no one knows who Guiseppe Croff is. And that's because his sculpture is a highly accomplished but largely derivative example of the academic style of the period. He is, in a word, a talented and gifted craftsman, who nevertheless failed to create original art.

But this is not to say that Warhol provides aid and comfort to the champions of simulacral culture. You call him a "Pop" artist, but that is a term more accurately applied to someone like Peter Max, who sold massively in the 1960s and 70s precisely because he valorized the most vapid clichés of his time.

No one in Warhol's America wanted to be told that their country was a collection of mass-produced Campbell soup cans, blood-splattered Jackies, or ghoulish electric chairs, but the youth culture of the period took it as a matter of faith that psychedelic love would transform the world into utopia. Max's immensely successful "Love" poster—which sold thousands—delivered precisely that feel-good message. It was the Pietà of the period, bringing a cannabis-laced aura to every dorm-room in America.

JS: I don't like the way Warhol has it both ways: sneering at vulgarity and laughing all the way to the bank as he mass-produces that vulgarity. Flaubert's lyricizing of vulgarity is memorable because he spent five years writing *Madame Bovary*, often working ten to twelve hours per day. Surely Warhol's manipulation of his vulgar idiom will have no lasting appeal. It is the creature of fashion and caprice, willfully so. I agree that *Veiled Nun* is aca-demic and derivative. But it is not a collection of soup cans that one can look at for two seconds, get the joke, and then glide away on museum-legs to pretend to care about the next travesty of art.

RB: Is the test of aesthetic value how much time the artist put in? Dr. Johnson could rip off a *Rambler* faster than most caffeine-crazed bloggers can construct a paragraph. Mozart composed symphonies in half the time the average rock musician spends writing a song. Voltaire, Goethe, Dickens, Picasso, Stravinsky and Pound all created with amazing rapidity and dexterity. But this is irrelevant. Surely we judge art on the results, not how quickly or slowly it was produced?

I have no idea whether Warhol laughed, cried, smirked or smiled on the way to the bank, and I don't much care. Though I am pleased he was well paid for his art, which is rarely the case. You say that Warhol will have "no lasting appeal," but we are now some twenty-five years out from his death, and his reputation continues to rise. Certainly his work is not merely a "creature of fashion," since the fashions he was critiquing are long forgotten. One need only turn to Peter Max to see how out-of-date a real "creature of fashion" looks today.

Is Warhol an artist of the first order? Probably not. But for my money he is an important artist of the second order, which is no mean accomplishment, and I would bet he will still be hanging in museums fifty years hence—if we still have museums. And it is to that last point that I would like to turn. We have discussed how representation has moved from a Hellenic celebration of the surface to a Hebraic plumbing of the depths, from mechanical reproduction to digitalized simulacra, and I have asked several times if the technological revolution Benjamin identified has fundamentally changed our idea of art. I still remain unclear as to your response.

For me, the status of art has been profoundly transformed in our time, not entirely as a result of mechanical reproduction (and the simulacral culture that followed) but significantly aided and abetted by these changes. That transformation consists quite simply in contemporary culture having eroded—perhaps having eliminated—the distinction between *art* and *entertainment*. The former requires culture, education, time and taste, while the latter is instantly and effortlessly available to all. The former participates in tradition, while the latter is an expression of fashion. The former speaks to all times, while the latter speaks to one time and that an increasingly brief time (Warhol's "fifteen minutes"). The scar of Tina Fey will be forgotten tomorrow. The scar of Odysseus will last forever.

JS: Twenty-five years is not much. Dr. Johnson recommended one hundred years. I think that's about right because it means the work has survived caprice and fashion and has remained compelling. I don't at all disagree with your main point about how mechanical reproduction has vitiated art. Indeed, I maintain that is precisely what the "achievement" of Warhol demonstrates. I will never get my head or my heart around an artist who said, as Warhol did, "There's nothing so American as shopping and I am an American." And I am not in the least persuaded—although I steadfastly refuse to do the necessary "research"—that rock musicians labor over their compositions longer than Mozart did when he wrote, for example, *Symphony No. 25*. You must know of some profoundly assiduous rock musicians. I do not. I think of Warhol as important for showing just how far art has dropped into disrepute. If that was his point, then good for him. But it's a dead end.

I will get myself to a veiled nunnery and delight again and again (and again) in how Croff magically sculpted a veil and the face beneath at one go. That illusion of surface and depth continually enchants, even mesmerizes.

RB: My point regarding Mozart and Samuel Johnson was simply that the speed with which they composed tells us nothing about the quality of their art. You declined once again to take up the question of Benjamin and mechanical reproduction. Any final thoughts?

JS: Benjamin was prescient, no doubt, in his thinking. Pretty soon we will all be so "translated" into our computers and so obsessed with reproducing and digitizing ourselves and everything around us that we will utterly lack the sensitivity and moral intelligence to respond properly to the scar of Odysseus.

RB: Of course, Benjamin welcomed the Brave New World of mechanical reproduction. For him, better political engagement than cultic mystification, better Muni's *Scarface* than Odysseus' scar. From our present vantage, Benjamin's belief in the cinema as an extended exercise in Brechtian *Verfremdung* seems wildly naïve—a point Adorno himself made in a 1936 letter to Benjamin.

Then again, photography and the cinema are fully legitimate art forms that have now produced their own rich and varied histories. And lest we forget, movable type is itself a form of mechanical reproduction. Should we, perhaps, apply some Brechtian *Verfremdung* to ourselves? In *The Wizard of Oz*, the "man behind the curtain" is a symbol for Hollywood itself—all those spectacular effects are revealed to be nothing more than the by-product of *technē*. But isn't Croff's "woman behind the veil" herself the by-product of *technē*? Indeed, hasn't the illusion-making of art always depended on the craftsman's ability to use his tools to good effect? "Et ignotas animum dimittit artes" ("and he turned his mind to the obscure arts") Ovid says of Daedalus, and Joyce says of Stephen. Perhaps it is the labyrinth that most perfectly illustrates the interplay of Auerbachian surface and depth? Perhaps art has always feared becoming entrapped in its own technologies? But what's an artist to do? The wings he would use to escape are as much the product of *technē* as the labyrinth from which he seeks to escape.

JS: I respond to art precisely because it does not have a silly dog pulling aside its curtain—or veil. Croff chiseled both woman *and* curtain simultaneously. That form of *technē*, that sensitively, sensuously-tooled illusion, seems to me a felicitous acceptance of the artist's "croffmanship." Even labored puns—as you can see—love to take the veil, presenting two levels or layers at once. When Toto (the currish cynic) pulls aside the curtain to reveal the frantic Wizard, puffing and bellowing and wildly gesticulating, I lose all interest in Oz. Too much infrastructure.

RB: You have returned us to one of the unanswered questions with which I began, so let me re-ask it as we head toward a conclusion. Auerbach and Benjamin, both refugees from National Socialism, fled a culture dominated by the manipulation of beautifully deceptive and deceptively beautiful images. Albert Speer and Leni Riefenstahl were Hitler's Überwizards, and the Oz-like spectacles that they contrived had the effect of turning the Third Reich into a huge *Gesamtkunstwerk*. To what extent are Auerbach and Benjamin products of their own history, critics who seek to sensitize us to the lures of mystification, whether it is generated by seductive surfaces or cultic auras? Are they, like that other cynic, Bertolt Brecht, of Toto's party, employing alienation-effects to remind us that the man behind curtain—or maniac behind the veil—is simply pulling the strings on which we dance? Albert

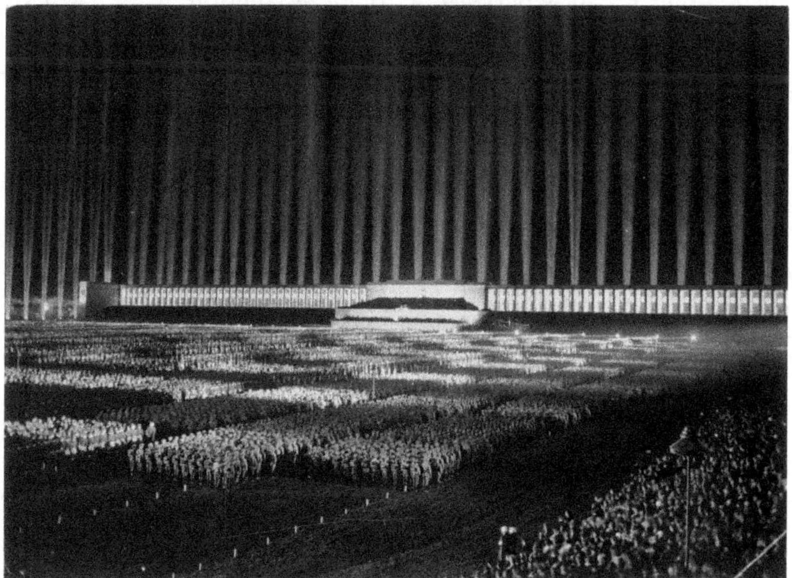

Figure 9: Albert Speer, *Lichtdom*.

Speer's "Cathedral of Light" from a 1930s Nuremberg rally was described by the then British Ambassador, Sir Nevile Henderson, as "both solemn and beautiful ... like being in a cathedral of ice." Where do we place it in relation to the Parthenon and Canterbury Cathedral, each of which, in their different ways, helped inspire it? And is it a "sensuously-tooled illusion" that we should sustain or destroy? Should we treat it as an icon, or should we treat it iconoclastically?

JS: Do we have any record of what Benjamin thought of Riefenstahl's *Triumph of the Will* (1935)? Is his famous essay of 1936 a cautionary meditation on the dangers of manufacturing aura, ritual and tradition for the beleaguered, hopeless masses? I think Benjamin must have loathed Riefenstahl's work as a perversion of his hope that art could revolutionize the masses away from fascism and toward communism.

We must recall Benjamin's famous last words in "The Work of Art in the Age of Mechanical Reproduction": "Mankind, which in Homer's time was an object of contemplation for the Olympian gods, now is one for itself. Its self-alienation has reached such a degree that it can experience its own destruction as an aesthetic pleasure of the first order. This is the situation of politics which Fascism is rendering aesthetic. Communism responds by politicizing art." But do we know precisely what Benjamin thought of Riefenstahl's work? Did he attack her in print before he died in 1940?

Finally, speaking of self-alienation and film, I sometimes wonder if our mass obsession with films about destruction (from cars blow-ing up to White Houses and Death Stars exploding) is contemporary culture's way of aestheticizing its death-instinct. *Thanatos* is so compellingly cinematic. We look down on our own calamitous destruction as if we were wistful Olympian gods, rather than part of the smoking, radioactive rubble: self-alienation copulating with self-delusion of the first order. To contemplate, through film, the ever-burgeoning nuclear "mushroom cloud" (two metaphors!—at once distancing and making familiar) is simultaneously to marvel at our godlike powers of creation and destruction and to drag back the curtain on our lethal wizardry.

This is what happens when we allow cinema to put a film over our eyes.

The closing sequence from *Dr. Strangelove* (1964) is a montage of mushroom clouds presented for our grimly ironic (iconic?) and satiric delectation. Annihilation as ersatz-melodrama is completed as Vera Lynn sings "We'll Meet Again" (1939) when it is pretty clear that the poor sods under those stunning mushrooms will never meet anyone again.

RB: Siegfried Kracauer, Benjamin's friend and colleague at the Frankfurt School, wrote an entire book on German film entitled *From Caligari to Hitler,* a book in which Riefenstahl figures briefly but significantly. Kracauer, Benjamin and Adorno were all fascinated by the new art of cinema, visited the UFA studios and discussed movies among themselves. Whether or not Benjamin saw *Triumph of the Will* after leaving Germany, he was certainly aware of Riefenstahl and what she represented.

Having said that, I think the stark summons that concludes "Mechanical Reproduction"—aesthetics *or* politics—poses a false choice. Any *genuine* aesthetic response demands that we both feel *and* understand—indeed, as Kant argues in "Analytic of the Beautiful," that we integrate these faculties—and that means that the serious critic never abandons reason or analysis. We can admire Riefenstahl's artistry and despise her politics, just as we can delight in the deftness with which Homer narrates Odysseus' scar, without losing sight of the violence that occasioned it.

The famous ending to *Dr. Strangelove* both aestheticizes politics (those mushroom clouds *are* lovely) and politicizes aesthetics (the irony of the Vera Lynn song is devastating). And Kubrick's ending, in its own way, perfectly illustrates the parable that gives our dialogue its title. Those hungry birds only experience Zeuxis' painting when it smacks them in the face. Genuine art breaks down, breaks apart, estranges habitual perception, thereby enabling us to *see anew*. The grape produced by *technē* both is and is not a grape. And it is in that strangely beautiful space where *is* and *is not* come together that art performs all of its Oz-like wizardry.

PART TWO:
EVIL, DEATH, LOVE, POLITICS

The Art of Darkness

JS: I think evil, like charity, begins at home. We know not what evil we do partly because "the family romance" that has invented us disguises our motives and makes us, in our own eyes, nearly indecipherable and therefore unaccountable. Poets try to decipher us. In the well-known words of the all-too-human Philip Larkin: "They fuck you up, your mum and dad / They may not mean to, but they do." Larkin's editorial conclusion is wistfully cautionary (it's worth noting and—one imagines—celebrating the fact that Larkin had no children):

> Man hands on misery to man.
> It deepens like a coastal shelf.
> Get out as early as you can,
> And don't have any kids yourself.

As a corrective to this spidery spleen, I recall that in *Heart of Darkness*, Marlow tells us "all of Europe went into the making of Kurtz," that he had splendid parents and lovely career possibilities, and that he still became one of the most impressively fucked-up figures in Western literature, nearly the epitome of evil. Where does evil come from? When and why may one not put the word "evil" in quotation marks? Is there a distinction between absolute and circumstantial evil? Even Hitler and Stalin were babies bouncing on parental knees before they began handing on misery to man. I am not overly-fond of the word "evil." It is too Christian. Pagans had no understanding of it, did they?

How to cite this book chapter:
Begam, R. and Soderholm, J. 2015. The Art of Darkness. In: Begam, R. and Soderholm, J. *Platonic Occasions: Dialogues on Literature, Art and Culture*. Pp. 59–80. Stockholm: Stockholm University Press. DOI: http://dx.doi.org/10.16993/sup.baa.d.

RB: I find the origins of evil mysterious. Does it begin at home? Perhaps. In the case of Kurtz—a sort of Raskolnikov with a pith helmet—what interests me is not his family history so much as his innate abilities. Marlow is unable to say "which was the greatest" of Kurtz's many talents and ends by describing him as a "universal genius." Surely it is no accident that in Genesis, Evil and Knowledge are eaten in the same apple; or that in Sophocles, Oedipus is not only the Breaker of Taboos but also the Unriddler of the Sphinx; or that in Goethe, Faust trades away his immortal soul to solve the mysteries of the universe. Certainly I believe that evil—without the quotation marks—is real. How frequently it flourishes (I deliberately use the Baudelairean metaphor) among the most active and curious minds. When Blake said Milton was of "the devil's party" was he speaking of himself—or of all those who dare to think what is forbidden?

JS: That the pedigreed imagination and the initiatives of evil are "kissing cousins" plays havoc with any hope for human beings or for the Humanities, largely conceived. I like to think—to hope—that the imagination is robustly antithetical to evil machinations. But perhaps we should see them as collaborative, conspiring partners. Artists and intellectuals are particularly good at dreaming up more and more baleful mischief. Bring out the Instruments of Torture. That means: bring out the Human Beings. What if—*horrible dictu*—*We* are Satan? After all, is there any rougher beast on the planet than what John Gray (in *Straw Dogs: Thoughts on Humans and Other Animals*) calls *homo rapiens*?

RB: Eve, Oedipus, Faust, Raskolnikov and Kurtz are all overreachers, whose desire for knowledge, especially the esoteric and proscribed kind, is so intense that they will sacrifice everything in pursing it. Literature gives us numerous examples of such characters, and their creators are among the greatest writers—from Dante, Shakespeare, Blake, Byron and Baudelaire to Dostoyevsky, Wilde, Proust, Conrad and Kafka. All these authors explored the hidden places of the human psyche, often lingering in its deepest and darkest recesses. Can *homo* be truly *sapiens* if he is not—at least a little—*rapiens*?

JS: As John Gardner wrote in *Grendel* (referring to man-animals), "No wolf was ever so cruel to other wolves." I once mentioned that line to him and he said, "Writers are even worse." I think he meant that writers and other artists can be terribly cruel in their imaginations, but also hard work for those around them. Perhaps all the time spent imagining scenes of evil (as Victor Frankenstein does) contaminates or poisons one's soul. Yet Mary Shelley was, unlike her husband, a real sweetheart. Percy used his genius to write lyric poetry about Love and the Imagination and treated Mary—and many others—as hired help. Both Shelleys explore the hidden places you mention (two versions of Prometheus) but, oddly enough, the darker imagination (Mary's) does nothing to pollute its author's moral sensibility. And for all Percy's soaring lyrics about Love Unbound, he was often a complete bastard. What, if anything, can we conclude, or wildly surmise?

RB: Whether the Promethean fires are banked low or high, whether the Vulture of the Caucuses feeds ill or well, artists' moral sensibilities are bound neither by the darkness of their vision nor the extremity of their experience. You observed elsewhere that we must judge works of art case by case, and I think that applies to artists as well. Having said that, I am nevertheless struck by how much sympathy for the Devil there is among writers. Perhaps this—what to call it?—aesthetic Satanism is simply a romantic and/or modernist conceit. Then again, all of Greek tragedy, much of the Bible, and a great deal of Western literature from the Renaissance to the French Revolution is attracted to Evil and its sinister machinations.

Oscar Wilde famously wrote in the Preface to *The Picture of Dorian Gray*:

> There is no such thing as a moral or an immoral book.
>
> Books are well written, or badly written. That is all.
>
> The nineteenth-century dislike of Realism is the rage of Caliban seeing his own face in a glass.
>
> The nineteenth-century dislike of Romanticism is the rage of Caliban not seeing his own face in a glass.
>
> The moral life of man forms part of the subject matter of the artist, but the morality of art consists in the perfect use of an imperfect medium.

We have two separate questions before us. What do we make of the evil of Kurtz when we think of him as a man—not a character? And what do we make of the evil of Kurtz when we think of him as a character—not a man?

JS: So long as literature stylizes evil (how could it not?) it also largely neutralizes its content. But if one were to come across a Kurtz "in real life" I suspect one would be alarmed, if not appalled, if not frightened half to death. Aesthetic Satanism is a kind of literary thought-experiment: a way of experimenting with evil, trying it on for size. Actual Satanism is no doubt far less appealing. Raging Caliban is a delight on stage, whether he is raging against seeing or not seeing his face in various glasses. If we were to meet Caliban in a dark alley or on a dark island, I suspect he would be rather less delightful. Perhaps we absorb evil in art partly to inoculate us against the real thing? Or is there something more baleful about aesthetic Satanism that I am missing?

We still have not discussed, moreover, what evil is. Doesn't it require some kind of (Christian?) metaphysics to get off the ground? When a dog pees on the kitchen floor, we say "bad dog, bad dog." We don't say "evil dog, evil dog." When Mrs. Goebbels poisons all six of her children in Hitler's bunker in Berlin, we say she is "evil." Why?

RB: Is Kurtz's evil absolute or relative? What, precisely, are his crimes? He has demonstrated skill, courage and ingenuity in leading a small band of men on raids in hostile territory. That he pillages, fights for material gain and takes trophies of war makes him no different from Agamemnon, Caesar, Henry V, Napoleon or Okonkwo. Indeed, what separates Kurtz from these celebrated figures are not his actions but our morals and—rather interestingly—his own. Caesar says, "Veni, vidi, vici." Kurtz says, "The horror! The horror!"

Remember that *virtue* comes from the Latin word for "man" (*vir, viris*), with all that implies regarding strength, courage and masculinity. It was in the European Middle Ages that *virtue*—an ideal that originally signified *virility*—was feminized and pietized into its opposite: chastity, grace, restraint. So Achilles was cast out by Jesus, as the man of action became the man of passion—the man who "passively" (*patior, passus sum*) forbears, endures, suffers.

Does the concept of evil require (Christian) metaphysics? Certainly Christianity was the driving force in transforming virtue from an active to a passive mode of conduct. But for Nietzsche, it was Judaism rather than Christianity that led to the "slave revolt" against "noble morality." The original opposition between Good and Bad was transposed into an opposition between Good and Evil, and in the process what had been esteemed (the noble, the powerful, the vigorous) was displaced by what had been reviled (the ignoble, the impotent, the feeble). The low became the high, the physically weak became the morally strong. As Nietzsche writes toward the end of the First Essay in *On the Genealogy of Morals*: "The two *opposing* values 'good' and 'bad,' 'good and evil' have been engaged in a fearful struggle on earth for thousands of years ... The symbol of this struggle, inscribed in letters legible across human history, is 'Rome against Judea, Judea against Rome.'" Kurtz has a Roman temperament which is finally undone by a Judean—or if you prefer Christian—conscience.

JS: I think Conrad invented Kurtz partly to make us wonder where the line is between "bad" and "evil" and between "bad" and "mad." Marlow's perturbed ambivalence about Kurtz—which grows as he gets closer (in both senses) to Kurtz—suggests just how blurry moral matters can be. Indeed, Marlow ends up backing Kurtz over the Manager. In his "choice of nightmares" he chooses Kurtz. The Manager is an inaesthetic Satan, a bureaucratic devil, a hollow man. It is the Manager who will end up in "real life" being a Himmler. At least Kurtz is remarkable and has some kind of genius clinging to his unspeakable rites and appetites. The Manager "originates nothing."

One is reminded of Hannah Arendt's comments at the end of *Eichmann in Jerusalem*. Here is how she describes Eichmann's final moments:

> When the guards tied his ankles and knees, he asked them to loosen the bonds so that he could stand straight. "I don't need that," he said when the black hood was offered him. He was in complete

> command of himself, nay, he was more: he was completely himself. Nothing could have demonstrated this more convincingly than the grotesque silliness of his last words. He began by stating emphatically that he was a *Gottgläubiger,* to express in common Nazi fashion that he was no Christian and did not believe in life after death. He then proceeded: "After a short while, gentlemen, *we shall all meet again*. Such is the fate of all men. Long live Germany, long live Argentina, long live Austria. *I shall not forget them.*" In the face of death, he had found the cliché used in the funeral oratory. Under the gallows, his memory played him the last trick: he was "elated" and he forgot that this was his own funeral.
>
> It was as though in those last minutes he was summing up the lesson that this long course in human wickedness had taught us—the lesson of the fearsome, word-and-thought-defying *banality of evil*.

Whatever gave Eichmann a feeling of elation, however momentary and clichéd, determined both his behavior and his beliefs. If the clichés were contradictory that did not trouble Eichmann so long as they inspired him. At least Kurtz does not traffic in clichés, unless one thinks of "The horror! The horror!" as the last words of a man hollowed out by his Judeo-Christian conscience. Is the "banality of evil"—and the evil of banality—what Absolute Evil has come to in the modern age: a democratization of Evil, what Alexander Pope predicted three-hundred years ago as "The Triumph of Dullness"?

RB: Nietzsche teaches us that morality is contingent, that Rome defines it one way and Judea another. Conrad shows us what that contingency looks like. Everyone knows Marlow's first words: "And this also has been one of the dark places of the earth." But do you remember his next utterance? "I was thinking of very old times, when the Romans first came here, nineteen-hundred years ago ..." Conrad opens his novella by staging Nietzsche's "fearful struggle" blazoned across "human history" between Rome and Judea:

> Imagine the feelings of a commander of a fine—what d'ye call 'em?—trireme in the Mediterranean, ordered suddenly to the north; run overland across the Gauls in a hurry; put in charge of

> one of these craft the legionaries used—a wonderful lot of handy men they must have been, too … Imagine him here … Sand-banks, marshes, forests, savages … Or think of a decent young citizen in a toga—perhaps too much dice, you know—coming out here in the train of some prefect, or tax-gatherer, or trader even, to mend his fortunes …

"Or trader even … to mend his fortunes." Kurtz is a cross between the legionary and the decent citizen, and seen from one perspective (that of Rome) he is a perfectly upstanding individual. But seen from another (that of Judea) he is just the opposite:

> They were conquerors, and for that you want only brute force—nothing to boast of, when you have it, since your strength is just an accident arising from the weakness of others. They grabbed what they could get for the sake of what was to be got. It was just robbery with violence, aggravated murder on a great scale … The conquest of the earth, which mostly means the taking it away from those who have a different complexion or slightly flatter noses than ourselves, is not a pretty thing when you look into it too much.

As for Conrad's bureaucratic Hollow Men—the Chief Accountant, the Manager and the Brick Maker—they are indeed examples of the banality of evil, men who originate nothing but keep the machinery of destruction oiled and operating. Eichmann dies unrepentant, persuaded to the last that he has done his duty and behaved as a good German. Kurtz, on the other hand, ends his days in horror and ignominy: "The voice was gone. What else had been there? But I am of course aware that next day the pilgrims buried something in a muddy hole."

You ask if Absolute Evil has been reduced to banality in our time. But hasn't evil always been banal? The executioners of the Inquisition were just as humanly inhuman as the guards at Dachau. They grumbled about the low pay, became bored with the routines of brutalization, and went home after a hard day of applying rack and thumbscrew to play with their children and fuck their wives. It is not simply the torturer's horse that scratches its innocent behind. The not-so innocent torturer scratches his as well. Could anything be more banal?

JS: It's worth noting that in Conrad's darkest novel about his darkest character he rarely uses the word "evil." Rather, he embeds or suggests it in its epithetical cousin, as we see here:

> I've seen the devil of violence, and the devil of greed, and the devil of hot desire; but, by all the stars! these were strong, lusty, red-eyed devils, that swayed and drove men—men, I tell you. But as I stood on this hillside, I foresaw that in the blinding sunshine of that land I would become acquainted with a flabby, pretending, weak-eyed devil of a rapacious and pitiless folly.

The adjective "flabby" has always given me pause. Kurtz's—and the Manager's—moral flabbiness is what makes them particularly unappealing. Perhaps, as you imply, there has always been something flaccid and shapeless about d/evils. The torturer is guilty of imaginative sloth in giving no mind to the exquisite pain of his victims. Has "evil" all along been a species of sloth? Edmund Burke's famous line comes to mind: "All that is required for evil to prevail is for good men to do nothing."

RB: In Salman Rushdie's *The Satanic Verses*, the narrator, having considered various explanations for why people commit evil, ends by proposing the following: "Let's rather say an even harder thing: that evil may not be as far beneath our surfaces as we like to say it is. —That, in fact, we fall towards it *naturally*, that is, *not against our natures*." In *Genealogy of Morals*, Nietzsche says a harder thing still: "To see others suffer does one good, to make others suffer even more: this is a hard saying but an ancient, mighty, human, all-too-human principle to which even the apes subscribe."

The emphasis falls differently in these two accounts. For Rushdie evil is inertial: it is our natural condition and rather than resist it (flabby devils that we are), we passively submit to its sinister attractions; whereas for Nietzsche, evil is kinetic: it appeals to our primitive instincts (red-eyed devils that we are), and we actively seek out its dark festival of violence and cruelty.

Flabby devil or red-eyed devil? Here is what T. S. Eliot writes in his essay, "Baudelaire": "So far as we are human, what we do must be either evil or good; and it is better, in a paradoxical way, to do evil than to do nothing; at least, we exist."

JS: It's hard not to recall in this context a famous moment from *Wuthering Heights*, when Heathcliff describes his red-eyed relish in tormenting the Lintons: "I have no pity! I have no pity! The more the worms writhe, the more I yearn to crush out their entrails! It is a moral teething; and I grind with greater energy in proportion to the increase of pain."

No wonder Bataille could get a chapter out of Emily Brontë in *Literature and Evil.* He writes: "I believe that the Evil—an acute form of Evil—which [literature] expresses, has a sovereign value for us. But this concept does not exclude morality: on the contrary, it demands a 'hypermorality.'" Heathcliff's "moral teething" is perhaps that hypermorality, as are the "unspeakable rites" of Kurtz. That we must imagine those rites makes the reader pleasurably complicit in them—Kurtz's semblance, his brother, his flowering evil twin.

RB: In the Preface to *The Nigger of the "Narcissus,"* Conrad observes that literature depends on "an impression conveyed through the senses," which means that the writer's task is "to make you hear, to make you feel ... before all, to make you *see*." Certainly if we apprehend with Kurtz's eyes and ears—if our hearts beat with his in the darkness—then at some level we become complicit in his evil. But it is no accident that both *Wuthering Heights* and *Heart of Darkness* give us, in Lockwood and Marlow, framing devices that mitigate any immediacy of impression. In effect, Brontë and Conrad make us readers "see" our own "seeing"—which is to say, they make us conscious of our complicity—and this manipulation of sympathy and distance is crucial to any moral understanding of these novels.

Bataille asserts that "Hypermorality is the basis of that challenge to morality which is fundamental to *Wuthering Heights*." Conrad writes a novel that contemplates in the figure of Kurtz a genuine "hypermorality," a Nietzschean *jenseits* that seeks to stand above or beyond morality, thereby enabling the "transvaluation of all values." But I think only a lapsed Catholic like Bataille—obsessed with Sade, Satanism and human sacrifice—would re-imagine Emily Brontë as the mustachioed German philosopher, unblinkingly staring into the abyss and discovering there the outer limits of morality. Heathcliff is simply one of Byron's dark avengers, with all the Sympathy for the Devil that implies. But neither he nor Brontë philosophizes with a hammer.

JS: The manipulation of sympathy and distance you mention and the question of the author's and the reader's complicity in the "evil" of the literary text are precisely what emerges from any discussion of the value of Blake's observation that "Milton is of the devil's party without knowing it." I defend Blake's reading to students and then show that Milton knows and advertises his "complicity" with evil (epically, heroically and finally ironically) in ways that make him ultimately *not* of the devil's party. *That* is how Milton transvalues the values he inherits from both the Judeo-Christian tradition and the classical tradition (Homer, Virgil). He transumes—as Bloom would say—the hell out of his predecessors. He hammers away until Satan's "Evil, be thou my Good" is made into a transparently ludicrous piece of rhetorical buffoonery. To read Satan's braying in hell as a Promethean, titanic affirmation of rebellion and individualism (the Romantic reading) is to be deaf (or blind) to Milton's subtle evocation of pride, temptation and sin in his epic performance. *Paradise Lost* invites us to repeat the Fall (including Milton's fall into the sin of poetic pride) over and over. That it does so cannily and cunningly suggests that Milton knows what he's about.

RB: Certainly, as Stanley Fish has argued, Milton wants the reader to be "surprised by sin"—to fall as fully as Adam and Eve—and like Brontë and Conrad he manipulates sympathy and distance to show how seductive the Devil can be. I also agree that *Paradise Lost* radically rewrites the epic tradition and, incidentally, does so in ways that perfectly correspond to Nietzsche's Rome vs. Judea formulation. What, according to Milton, would have been the most heroic act of all time? It would have consisted in Eve's *not* eating the apple, in Eve's doing *nothing*. To substitute inaction for action, forbearance for achievement, is fundamentally to reconceive what it means to be a hero. Imagine an Achilles who permits himself to be slain by Hektor and then, breathing his last, says "Forgive him Father, for he knows not what he does." Milton has not merely rewritten Homer and Virgil. He has Christianized them and the entire literary tradition they represent.

I am less convinced, however, that Milton delivers us to a hypermorality that stands beyond good and evil. By getting the reader to identify with Adam and Eve he reminds us that we are all fallen—that sin is our natural condition—but he does not treat ethical values as relative or contingent. To the contrary, Milton is as much a moral absolutist as Kant.

Conrad, on the other hand, gives us something different, a Satan who genuinely transcends moral values: "There was nothing either above or below him, and I knew it. He had kicked himself loose of the earth. Confound the man! He had kicked the very earth to pieces. He was alone, and I before him did not know whether I stood on the ground or floated in the air." Marlow brings us closer to Kurtz than Lockwood does to Heathcliff. In a state of existential vertigo, Marlow begins to lose his own moral footing, and as he floats free of the earth so does the reader. This is also the case with Kurtz's descent into the abyss. As Marlow remarks: "His was an impenetrable darkness. I looked at him as you peer down at a man who is lying at the bottom of a precipice where the sun never shines." But Marlow's gaze is not merely sympathetic—it is empathetic—and in following Kurtz into the depths, he carries the reader with him: "Since I had peeped over the edge myself, I understand better the meaning of his stare, that could not see the flame of the candle, but was wide enough to embrace the whole universe, piercing enough to penetrate all the hearts that beat in the darkness." In the end, Conrad's darkness, like Joyce's snow, is general: it falls through the universe upon all the living and the dead.

And yet, if I am right—if Conrad's novel really does contemplate a hypermorality—then what do we make of its conclusion? If the universe is nothing more than a bottomless abyss of darkly beating hearts, why does Marlow lie to the Intended? Why not tell her the truth? Kurtz's last words were not the cherished name of his beloved, but "The horror! The horror!"

JS: I suppose you could argue that Conrad teases himself (and the reader) with the hypermorality of a heartfelt darkness and then pulls back and retrenches himself in the "white lie" to the Intended. Marlow needs to keep women in an unreal, illusory, fairytale world. That he lies to her at all, knowing how much lies are like biting into mortality (Eve's eating death in the form of an apple) suggests an asymptotic approach to the "higher" morality associated with the devilish Kurtz. The novelist giveth, and the novelist taketh away. In living through Kurtz's "extremity," Marlow pushes the reader into the same position, and we begin to contemplate the possibility that all facts are, as Michael Levenson claims, "value-laden." And those values, like customs and conventions, can change.

Underneath the house where I write to you are remnants of the Roman wall that those first soldiers erected after they invaded Britain, cheerfully building straight roads and easily foisting their values—and their language—on the locals. And then Judea cast out Rome, using those straight roads to spread the word. Where does this leave us?

RB: A Roman wall and Christian cathedral. Call it the Archaeology of Morals. And yet you began the dialogue by asking if it possible to liberate "evil" from its quotation marks, to speak of it not as archaeological or genealogical but as absolute. Inevitably, a few pages later, Adolph Eichmann made his appearance.

Perhaps the time has come to confront Caliban not as a fictional creation but as an historical reality. So let me now re-ask the question that has hovered over this dialogue from the outset. Were the perpetrators of the Holocaust contingently evil, circumstantially evil, relatively evil—however we wish to describe it—or were they Evil, full stop?

JS: I think "the horror" is the strong implication that when Kurtz writes, in his post-script, "Exterminate all the brutes," he is referring *at once* to the savages in the Congo *and* the savages from Belgium who are exploiting them. What follows from that grim ambiguity is the fact that *all* "evil" is circumstantial, including Nazi evil. A chicken farmer in Germany in 1932, down on his luck, poor, with no national pride or personal pride, can in 1942 be devising more and more efficient ways to exterminate

European Jewry. That is not pure evil. It is contingent, circumstantial, historically-specific evil. In the "right" situation, the sweetest, Rousseau-incubated creatures on the planet might turn into Hobbesian monsters. I think "pure evil" is a simplification—and reification—of contingent evil. Do you disagree?

RB: If there is such a thing as pure evil, then the Death Camps are certainly an example of it. Dante merely imagined Hell. The Nazis built it. A number of years ago I read a newspaper article describing an indescribable crime. A man picked up a woman hitchhiker, raped her, cut off her hands and feet with an ax and then threw her bloody remains in a ditch by the freeway. The poor woman lived. To say that this crime is "contingently" or "historically" or "circumstantially" evil seems to miss the mark. The Holocaust is that crime raised to the power of six million.

When it comes to morals, I am not a Kantian, which is to say not a moral rigorist. Indeed according to the Prussian philosopher's categorical imperative, a Christian concealing Jews during World War II would be morally obliged to tell the truth if questioned by the Nazis. Why? Because moral actions must be guided by principles that could serve as "universal law," and as Kant points out, one "can by no means will a universal law of lying." On the other hand, the philosopher also enjoins us to act in such a way that we "treat humanity … never simply as a means, but always as an end." Kant would therefore condemn the Nazis for exterminating the Jews (treating them as a means) and condemn the Christian for lying about the Jews (to save them from being treated as a means). There is a lovely, mad logic to it all, but at the end of the day it makes more sense in theory than in practice.

Having said that, I can't agree with you about chicken farmer—and *Reichsführer*—Himmler. There were plenty of people in the great Depression who were down on their luck, had no personal or national pride and (lest we forget) were terminally awkward around women. But they didn't murder six million people because they were having a bad life. Can we really say that Himmler's evil is "circumstantial?" Isn't it an example of the purest, most unvarnished evil that has ever existed?

JS: I think "pure evil" must be a theological term if it is to make sense, at least to me. It is a form of evil that has eternal consequences for those who commit it. That is to say, pure evil must be different in *kind*, not just *degree*, from circumstantial evil. Or it is a kind of rhetorical trump card used to make the case of the Nazis seem uniquely evil. But I think "pure evil" is actually a higher degree of "circumstantial evil," so egregiously high that it seems different in kind and therefore "unvarnished." But all evil is necessarily varnished by a hugely complicated set of historical and biographical forces. This is not to excuse or exonerate its perpetrators in any way. It is rather to deliver them over to historians, sociologist, psychologists and legal tribunals—not to theologians (or Prussians) who would condemn them to one Hell or another.

RB: Since neither of us believes in God, neither of us believes in sin. The evil we are discussing does not depend on burning bushes or smoking tablets. Nevertheless, the question remains as to whether that evil is historically circumscribed. Anti-Semitism was rife throughout Europe in the 1930s and 1940s. But the Danes heroically resisted the persecution of the Jews, as did many Christians in Norway, Holland, France and, yes, Germany. Beckett risked his life fighting the Nazis and was later decorated with the *Croix de Guerre*. Picasso, when asked by a German officer if he was responsible for *Guernica*, responded "No, you are!" And after Hitler became *Reichskanzler* in 1933, Schoenberg, in a highly public act, reconverted to Judaism. People had choices and some chose good, while others chose evil.

But—you will press me—are we talking about circumstantial evil or pure evil? I suppose one way to answer this question is to ask how universalizable are the choices that the Holocaust presented. The mass murder of women and children, medical experiments including forced castrations and hysterectomies, the showers, the ovens, the piles of shoes, the mountains of hair, the emaciated rag-bodies bulldozed into mass graves. Would Nietzsche's aristocratic warrior have sanctioned such crimes? Would Achilles, Caesar, Okonkwo? Would Kurtz?

JS: Ours is becoming a terminological debate that must pale before the horror of the atrocities you mention. What finally hangs on determining if mass murder is an example of "pure" or "circumstantial" evil? I like to be precise about language and categories—as you do—but there's something a bit caviling (or scholastic, perhaps) about the distinction we are disagreeing about. I suppose I want to pin down not so much the *what* regarding evil but the *why*. Why were many Germans in the 1930s capable of mass murder (or turning a blind eye to it)? If I could go back in history and kill one man, it would be Himmler. He strikes me as particularly cold, bureaucratic, fatuous and repellent. Goebbels is a close second. But when it comes to understanding *why* people turn out to be so balefully hideous, I run up against a wall that not even the most assiduous historian or psychoanalyst can help me surmount.

RB: I think our disagreement is more substantive than you do. Insofar as certain crimes are condemned by virtually all cultures and ethical systems, they constitute "universally sanctioned" prohibitions. Viewed from this perspective, the Nazi atrocities are not contingently or historically evil, but evil in all times and all places. Still, as you point out, that leaves us to grapple with the fact that in the 1940s many Germans either participated in, or were complicitous with, mass murder.

In 1996, Daniel Goldhagen published a book entitled *Hitler's Willing Executioners*, which argued that ordinary Germans took part in the Holocaust because they were profoundly anti-Semitic. The book generated a critical firestorm and was roundly condemned by historians as Germanophobic. I have not waded into the deep waters of Holocaust studies, but even if we acknowledge that there are factual errors and questionable analyses in the book, its central thesis cannot be easily dismissed. Of course, it is no surprise that Goldhagen's commonsensical argument has proven anathema to many professional historians, who have blamed the Holocaust on everything from a bad economy (war reparations and hyperinflation) to the collapse of democracy (the end of the Weimar Republic), the conspiracy of a few Nazis (Reinhard Heydrich and the Wannsee conference) and (my personal favorite) the rise of anti-communism.

But if we assume that Goldhagen is right, then we may begin to make sense out of not only the Holocaust but any number of other atrocities in human history. What makes it possible for humans to commit horrific crimes—crimes that are universally condemned—is the simple belief that certain people are not fully human. Christians are fed to lions, Africans are impressed into slavery and Jews are sent to the ovens, because they are regarded as subhuman. And if they are subhuman, then we may treat them—to speak the language of Kant—not as ends but as means. They become vehicles for providing cheap labor, for harvesting the gold in their teeth and the hair on their head, even for entertaining a coliseum of bored Romans with a taste for spectacle and blood sport.

JS: Did all of Europe go into the making of the Holocaust? It seems to me that our dialogue may have come full circle. Larkin writes that "Man hands on misery to man. / It deepens like a coastal shelf." This is to generalize the problem of evil and to suggest that Hobbes and not Rousseau understood what human beings are really all about—that there's a little bit of "the horror" in all of us. For complicated reasons, bored Romans and excited Germans pushed their rapaciousness to lethal extremes. I think I take a much dimmer view of human beings than you do. Since the Holocaust, there have been arguably over thirty genocides, including Bangladesh (1971), East Timor (1975–1999), Cambodia (1975–1979), Guatemala (1981–1983), Bosnia (1992–1995), Rwanda (1994), Darfur and Sudan (2004 – present). There will be more.

When we are not being nice to each other and going to the theatre and cinema, we are at each other's throats, passing on our misery. Why? Because our mums and dads fucked us up, as they were fucked up in their turn? We are the evil we decry. Wipe the planet clean of humans and let the hopping, humping rabbits inherit the earth.

RB: There is much to be said for your Swiftian assessment of humanity, but I think matters are more complicated. You cite Birkin's nihilistic pronouncement from *Women in Love*, where he gleefully imagines the destruction of all mankind, "a world empty of people, just uninterrupted grass, and a hare sitting up." And yet, by the end of the novel Birkin and Ursula have fallen in love and are planning a trip to Verona, where they will sit in the amphitheatre and "find Romeo and Juliet." From nihilist to sentimentalist in a few hundred pages. All it took was a little star-equilibrium love. Of course, their idyll is interrupted by the arrival of Gerald's frozen corpse, and Lawrence's dark tango of *erōs* and *thanatos* continues. The Dance of Life capers with the Dance of Death in an endless round of creation and destruction.

What makes it all happen? Our parents? Our genes? Our stars? Ourselves? Do we drink in the life force and death drive with our mother's milk? Is that the Forbidden Knowledge that Eve first tastes and that Faust, Raskolnikov and Kurtz all pursue in their different ways? You said earlier that it is the historian, sociologist and psychologist who can best help us understand the problem of evil. What about the poet? Here is a passage from Paul Celan's "Death Fugue," which rewrites Genesis, Goethe's *Faust*, the Song of Solomon and the Holocaust as a single event, a mad orgy of birth, love and death:

> Black milk of daybreak we drink you at night
> we drink you at noon and in the morning we drink you in the evening
> we drink and drink
> a man lives in the house your golden hair Margarete
> your ashen hair Shulamith he plays with snakes
> he calls out play more sweetly death death is a master from Germany
> he calls out play more darkly the violins then you will rise as smoke in the air
> then you will have a grave in the clouds where you can spread out …

JS: That "grave in the clouds" is misery's "coastal shelf," deepening. Just as our horror becomes intolerable, "art may arrive," Nietzsche says, "as a saving sorceress, expert at healing." W. B. Yeats understood the "terrible beauty" of violence and the necessity to fabricate artifice even as Ireland's "civil war" (oxymoron grimly accepted) was offering a premonition of yet another Hobbesian *bellum omnium contra omnes.*

A barricade of stone or of wood;
Some fourteen days of civil war;
Last night they trundled down the road
That dead young soldier in his blood:
Come build in the empty house of the stare.

We had fed the heart on fantasies,
The heart's grown brutal from the fare;
More substance in our enmities
Than in our love; O honey-bees,
Come build in the empty house of the stare.

I take some little satisfaction in knowing that in a few million years, human beings—and their bloody, raging history of Calibanism—will have vanished from the planet, leaving it to the birds and the bees and the gently erect rabbits.

RB: Mankind is capable of extraordinary good, extraordinary evil and extraordinary beauty. Such is the human all-too-human condition, and I certainly prefer it to the innocent and—I might add—artless birds, bees and bunnies. Your green-dream of a *Menschenfrei* world strikes me as a nightmare of banality.

JS: "The mind of man is capable of anything because everything is in it—all the past as well as all the future." That is Marlow's dubious Gospel. It allows a glover's son to become Shakespeare. And it also allows a farmer's son to become a Jew-hating Nazi. There is neither rhyme nor reason to humanity or human behavior. The only way to make people "good" rather than "evil" is constantly to threaten them with punishment if they get out of line. Here are the hilarious and horrifying last lines of Flannery O'Connor's *A Good Man Is Hard To Find*: "'She would of been a good woman,' The Misfit said, 'if there had been somebody there to shoot her every minute of her life.'"

RB: O'Connor is right. People behave not because they should, but because they must. Which is to say, the Flowers of Good are best cultivated not in broad daylight but in the shadow of the prison-house and the gallows.

But what of those other umbral blossoms, the Flowers of Evil? Baudelaire reminds us that the most exquisite beauty is often born out of vileness and depravity. We began our dialogue by wondering about the relation between ethics and aesthetics, a topic we have touched upon elsewhere. Both Conrad and Celan produced great art—gorgeous flowers—out of horrific suffering. Obviously their depiction of suffering in no way redeems—to use a Conradian word—the experiences of those who perished in the Congo or the Death Camps. But is there a sense in which their art, by imaginatively transmuting those experiences, redeems mankind? You say there is "neither rhyme nor reason to humanity." But when we perfectly imperfect humans apply rhyme and reason to the horror that is our history—when we make art out of darkness—don't we in some measure tip the balance back in our favor, bring a little light to the dark night of the soul?

JS: I am reminded of one of the most profound lines in *King Lear*: "The worst is not / So long as we can say 'This is the worst.'" So long as we can articulate evil and despair, we are not yet at rock bottom, a place of darkness so complete that, like a black hole, neither light nor *logos* escape it. To return to our Conradian title, so long as there *is* an "art of darkness," then evil, suffering and "The horror! The horror!" are comfortably locked up in the prison-house of Language. But Kurtz goes in for some "unspeakable rites." What is beyond the pale of language, what is beyond even Conrad's visually-redemptive art, are acts of evil that beggar expression, visions of depravity so horrible that they cut the tongue out of the artist so that the rape cannot be given voice. Is that why we are told there "can be no poetry after Auschwitz"?

RB: "No poetry after Auschwitz," and yet we have Paul Celan, Primo Levi, Elie Wiesel and Imre Kertész—to mention only these. Franz Kafka famously commented to Max Brod, there is "hope … no end of hope—only not for us." He was speaking of God, and although he died before the Holocaust he correctly predicted that there would be no messianic deliverance for the Jews of Europe. Of his three sisters, two perished in the Lodz ghetto, and the third and youngest, Ottla, was executed at Auschwitz. She arose as "smoke in the air" and made her "grave in the clouds." Do Celan's words—his art—help mitigate the darkness that Ottla and so many others suffered? They did not help Celan, who committed suicide in 1970. But what of us? Is there hope for us?

Perhaps as we conclude this dialogue we can agree that evil—at least some kinds—cannot be fathomed. But it can be articulated—however tentatively, however imperfectly. Is that enough?

JS: Enough for what? To satisfy our aesthetic sense? To supply some sort of secular "redemption"? But one could argue that articulating evil, even artistically (particularly artistically?) only adds to the sum of evil in the world by giving it another mode of being—just as pity, Nietzsche observed, only adds to the sum of suffering in the world.

Finally, I don't believe in "evil" except as a metaphysical or religious construct designed to pedigree what is truly "bad" and give it eternal consequences. Perhaps there is a reason why Conrad never calls Kurtz "evil." I feel more and more uncomfortable using the word "evil" when what I am really referring to are forms of human depravity that require far more terminological subtlety and complexity, the kind that artists so richly supply: the "black milk" of lyric suggestiveness that flows, as Conrad would have it, into "the heart of an impenetrable darkness." I don't think art redeems anything, least of all "evil," but I do think it keeps us off the streets—or out of the jungle—and, while we are either creating it or consuming it, makes it slightly less likely that we will exterminate the brutes, whoever they happen to be.

RB: If our goal is merely something that will "keep us off the streets," then I should think bowling alleys and skating rinks would serve just as well as art.

As for our terminological debate, humans need a vocabulary for talking about the nasty things we do to each other. "Black milk" and "heart of darkness" are evocative metaphors that enable us to make emotional and ethical sense (rhyme and reason) out of horrific experiences. But when we are confronted with real-world choices, when we have to decide whether Eichmann should live or die, we require terms that are more conceptually precise than "dark heart" or "black milk."

JS: Courts of law do not pass judgments based on "evil" behavior. I think the word "evil" is avoided in jurisprudence—even in the Nuremberg trials—because it smuggles a kind of metaphysical vocabulary into the courtroom, when more conventional and secular terms such as "right" and "wrong" are sufficient to deprive the Nazi of his life. I would rather leave it to artists and poets to supply us with image after horrifying image of the accelerating grimace of our disastrous twentieth century.

The most recent grimace (pushing us along into the twenty-first century) may be Cormac McCarthy's *The Road*, an updating of Conrad's art of darkness in a post-apocalyptic America on the verge of becoming a place where my blessedly randy rabbits will, in a thousand years or two, inherit the earth. If only evolution would stop *there*—before the rabbits start to lust after the warren in the next field. But, alas, one day a miserable rabbit will grow into John Updike, another into Joseph Stalin, and the whole mammalian process will eternally return until Larkin's coastal shelf has deepened into something even oubliettes fear.

RB: Eichmann and the Nuremberg defendants were not charged with "evil" but with crimes against humanity. But "crimes against humanity" is a hell of a lot broader and vaguer than "larceny," "burglary" or "murder," and such a charge necessarily raises the question of what evil is and how we adjudicate and punish it. I might add that transcripts for both the Eichmann and Nuremberg trials show that the word "evil" was repeatedly used by prosecuting attorneys and presiding judges. Despite popular cynicism, there *is* a connection between ethics and secular law, and that connection goes to the heart of whether "evil" by definition involves Judeo-Christian metaphysics.

Every culture stigmatizes certain kinds of behavior with a severity that transcends what is simply "bad," and the word we use to describe such behavior is "evil." The Judeo-Christian history that stands behind the word neither determines nor defines its semantic content. Which is to say, evil is not necessarily a religious category. But even as a non-religious category, evil need not be a relative term. All cultures prohibit murder. Notions of right and wrong differ from place to place and time to time, but certain forms of criminality are universally condemned.

I wonder if our disagreement finally comes down to a debate between nature and culture. To what degree does the latter—where we locate things like art—insulate us against the former? I detect in your argument a certain Rousseauian nostalgia, a belief that human competition and struggle (criticized in Rousseau's *Second Discourse*) inevitably lead to the rapacity and criminality Conrad describes. If the bunnies could remain bunnies and the noble savages could remain nobly savage, then all would be well. You would happily sacrifice the Updikes in order to be spared the Stalins. I myself am a Hobbesian who feels that our best protection against the heart of darkness is civilization, with its discontents and imperfections, as well as its consolations. Presumably McCarthy and Conrad agree?

JS: I think McCarthy and Conrad would agree that human beings are capable of absolutely anything under certain circumstances. At the heart of the art of darkness is the unfathomable "The horror! The horror!"—a doublet that says less about the "evil" of Kurtz and more about language's expressive limits. But before we reach those limits, Conrad certainly gives us a banquet of nightmares that shows just how abominable human beings can be when teased by a whiff of ivory.

RB: As Michael Levenson says, "Vague terms still signify." If we cannot name evil—if we cannot identify it—then we cannot oppose it. "Evil" is imprecise, but I think we need it just as we need other vague terms, such as Good, Beauty and Art.

We are suspicious of such words, because they are value-laden and therefore demand that we make judgments. Marlow says of Kurtz's final pronouncement, "he had summed up—he had judged." I agree that "The horror! The horror!" is unfathomable, devoid of meaning. In other words, in the end Kurtz does *not* judge but takes refuge in a cliché. But for Conrad, we the reader—Kurtz's *semblable* and *frère*—we *must* judge. Otherwise it would be, to quote Marlow's last words, "too dark—too dark altogether."

Let's Hang Ourselves Immediately! On Death and Suicide

JS: I am never not thinking about suicide and death. Two remarks, a pair of dice, tumble across my consciousness. One: "The thought of death wonderfully concentrates the mind" (Dr. Johnson) and Two: "The thought of death gets one through many long nights" (Nietzsche). I long ago understood that Absurdity (à la Camus) not Morbidity was my life-blood and somehow that writing was the only way I could deal with the incandescent consciousness of the certainty of death. Death became for me a life-sentence, a huge collection of life-sentences. I suppose that is why *Hamlet* has emerged as the cause and effect of my death-haunted life. Hamlet in the graveyard, cupping Yorick's skull, staring into the abyss and making infinitely sad jests about our mortal condition, has been the alpha and omega of my imagination. That the sound and fury of life end up "signifying nothing" seems to me at once "The horror! The horror!" and part of the "final soliloquy of the interior paramour." To keep signifying nothing. That also sounds like a Beckettian *raison d'être*. To keep staining the silence. Not to stain is not to be. About nothing there must be much ado. And is not a dialogue also part of the will to stain the silence? We exchange (night) thoughts to give ourselves the impression we exist.

RB: Your dice—one thinks of Mallarmé—rattle like eloquent bones, but the topic of death and suicide leaves me as cold as camphor. Certainly there are cases where it makes sense to kill oneself, and I will happily defend the right of anyone to shuffle off this mortal coil. But I find it difficult to take seriously the romance of suicide. Hamlet's Melancholia, Werther's *Weltschmerz* and Camus's

---

How to cite this book chapter:
Begam, R. and Soderholm, J. 2015. Let's Hang Ourselves Immediately! On Death and Suicide. In: Begam, R. and Soderholm, J. *Platonic Occasions: Dialogues on Literature, Art and Culture*. Pp. 81–94. Stockholm: Stockholm University Press. DOI: http://dx.doi.org/10.16993/sup.baa.e.

Absurdity strike me as blinds, convenient vehicles for transforming the errors and insufficiencies of youth into existential crises. Once we push through the metaphysical posturing, what we discover in all three cases is personal failure of one kind or another. Hamlet failed to be a good Prince, Werther failed to be an adequate lover and Camus failed to fight the Nazis—at least, with any success. Rather than confront their own deficiencies, they constructed philosophies in which their impotence is the fault not of themselves but of the universe.

Byron, on the other hand, takes a more jaundiced view of young men who seek refuge in metaphysics:

> 'Twas strange that one so young should thus concern
> His brain about the action of the sky;
> If *you* think 'twas philosophy that this did,
> I can't help thinking puberty assisted.
>
> (*Don Juan* I, 93)

JS: I don't think there's anything particularly pubescent about Hamlet's meditations about death. Both Seneca and Montaigne trickle through his mortal reflections and pedigree his death-haunted consciousness. The Byronic squib you cite is clever enough but lofts us into matters metaphysical. Like you, I am not concerned with the romance of suicide (a strictly literary affair), but with the question of authenticity, Heidegger's Being-towards-death. Hamlet anticipates that authenticity in his tragic-comic remarks in the graveyard scene. Unlike Shakespeare, Heidegger never seems to find any humor whatsoever in our mortal condition. Hamlet's darkest pun—that Yorick is "quite chopfallen"—suggests that one can be both exquisitely sad and hilarious at the same time. That alloy is hard-won and, it seems to me, hardly juvenile. Hamlet is leagues beyond the simpering sorrows of young Werther.

RB: When I speak of the "romance of suicide," I am responding to the celebrated opening to *The Myth of Sisyphus*: "There is but one truly serious philosophical problem and that is suicide." A godless universe is an "absurd" universe, Camus claims, where meaning, value and truth have ceased to exist and where man labors endlessly at a futile task and then dies. Camus believes that human mortality is a problem, because—despite his atheism—he still accepts Christianity's central assumption: that Being and Time are antithetical. The classic statement of this position comes from Plato, but it enjoys an afterlife in both Neoplatonism and Christianity. Simply stated, this position holds that it is only through the Soul that we can experience true Being, because true Being is Timeless and the Soul alone enables us to lift ourselves out of Time.

All of this changes in 1927, when Heidegger publishes his *magnum opus* and turns Platonic ontology on its head. His argument is that *Sein und Zeit*—Being and Time—are not only inseparable (note the pun in the German) but in some important sense indistinguishable. Indeed, it is only through *Zeitlichkeit* ("temporality") that man experiences Being, or as Heidegger would say that *Sein* is disclosed to *Dasein*. On this reading, mortality is not the problem of the human condition but its solution—what confers significance, however contingent, on our three-score ten. As Heidegger (and Nietzsche) observe, an eternal life—one that requires no choices—would be a mere procession of events, a tedium of parataxis.

So my argument is that Camus, Werther and, yes, even Hamlet, romance suicide out of a Christianity that they themselves don't entirely understand. The "absurdity" of mortality is a fiction invented by the Church. A good pagan like Lucretius grasped this fact.

JS: Then how do you characterize the absurdity of Estragon and Vladimir wanting to hang themselves immediately because they might enjoy a posthumous erection? It's not a Christian joke. It's not an existential joke. But it's one of the funniest and saddest lines in the play.

RB: Indeed. The exchange is funnily unhappy and unhappily funny:

> ESTRAGON: What about hanging ourselves?
> VLADIMIR: Hmm. It'd give us an erection.
> ESTRAGON: (*highly excited*). An erection!

VLADIMIR: With all that follows. Where it falls mandrakes grow. That's why they shriek when you pull them up. Did you know that?
ESTRAGON: Let's hang ourselves immediately!

As I read it, "Let's hang ourselves immediately" fully acknowledges Estragon and Vladimir's temporality—the fact that they exist in and through time—with a play on the Elizabethan pun: to die is not to go, but to come. Death is rhymed with Love, with its low points and high points, its anticipations and gratifications, its rising action, complications and final denouement. *Post coitum omne animal triste est. Et post vitam?* Who knows and who cares? Life is a performance and the final curtain a framing device. That the play ends betokens neither futility nor absurdity. Just narrative good sense.

JS: The entire play is Gogo and Didi hanging around. But to see the final curtain coming—to know with certainty it's coming: is not that where (or when) the sound and fury start to signify nothing in a way that, finally, is not edifying? As when Ivan Ilych, hanging curtains on some silly ladder, has his little fall and bruises himself unto death? It's not the fall into *mythos* and narrative plenitude that addles my night-thoughts. It's that sense of an ending when no artistic friskiness in the artificed world can keep the last syllable of recorded time from becoming the excruciating symphony of Ivan's three-day, mortal shriek.

RB: Rimbaud writes, "Comme je deviens vieille fille, à manquer du courage d'aimer la mort!" ["What an old lady I'm becoming, to lack the courage to love death!"]. Yes, most of us funk it in the end, and it's easier to talk about death as Lucretius might than to confront it squarely when it breathes its cold breath down our necks. But as much as death terrifies Ivan Ilyich, Tolstoy makes clear that his hero's struggle with mortality has improved him immeasurably. Ivan's fall is at once symbolic and fortunate. He is transformed from a petit bourgeois, preoccupied with card games and social gossip, into a fully sentient human being who actually comes to understand something of the life he must leave. Not only is the mind concentrated by death. It is formed by it.

Of course, *Waiting for Godot* is a play about two characters who attempt to turn *chronos* into *kairos*. They show us how suspended time can become redeemed time, not through the intervention of God the Father but by the pratfalls and hat tricks we invent while waiting for Him. So it is that *ousia* is produced out of an infinitely deferred *parousia*.

JS: I don't think Gogo and Didi "attempt" to do much of anything that resembles the heroic imperative of *kairos*. Rather than string the bow in the great hall, they puke away their puke of a life (*Kronos* devouring his kids and vomiting them) by stringing each other along, slack lyres, trying ever more desperately to strum their way through the next moment. Only Beckett could make this shameless and empty bantering, this yes yes no no yes yes, into a play of voices with ludic and lyric suggestiveness. In actual life—God[ot] help us—being trapped in *chronos* is rather less amusing. That life is a performance does little to sustain me. That art is a performance does something small to sustain me. My struggle with mortality may have improved me once. Now it makes me pratfall into sickly emotion.

RB: I am thinking not of "heroic" but of "significant" time. In *The Sense of an Ending*, Frank Kermode defines *chronos* as "passing" or "waiting time" and *kairos* as "a point in time filled with significance, charged with meaning derived from its relation to the end." In the Greek tradition, *kairos* is the "moment that must be grasped," and it is for that reason that the sculptor Lysippos represents him with a forelock that can symbolically be seized, as one seizes the day. Beckett plays with this tradition in *Murphy* when the narrator writes, "Let us now take Time ... bald though he be behind, by such few sad short hairs as he has." And in *Waiting for Godot*, when Vladimir urges that he and Estragon help a fallen Pozzo, it is precisely out of a desire to convert *chronos* into *kairos*: "Let us not waste our time in idle discourse! Let us do something, while we have the chance! It is not every day that we are needed. Not indeed that we personally are needed."

Beckett's play is an experiment in how humans transform "suspended" time into "redeemed" time. And that transformation occurs because "meaning" derives from our "sense of an ending." In the closing moments of *Waiting for Godot*, Vladimir soliloquizes in language reminiscent of Shakespeare: "Astride of a grave and a difficult birth. Down in the hole, lingeringly the grave-digger puts on the forceps." I like to imagine that Beckett is here thinking of the graveyard scene in *Hamlet*. Yorick is reborn out of Ophelia's grave, his skull tossed up by the grave-digger down in the hole. And just as Yorick has borne Hamlet on his shoulders, so Hamlet now bears Yorick in his hands. Death and birth go, as it were, hand-in-hand. They are the *Zeitlichkeit* that gives the "design" to *Dasein.*

You are fond of Hamlet's description of Yorick as "quite chopfallen," a dark pun that, as you say, combines the exquisitely sad and the hilariously funny. I'm partial to another moment of theatrical magic—when Hamlet calls Yorick "a fellow of infinite jest." As the audience witnesses Hamlet holding the skull, it becomes keenly aware of just how "finite" that jest was. Would those "flashes of merriment" have "set the table on a roar" had Yorick lived forever? Do the immortals laugh and cry at all? Or is theirs a life without care, pain or pleasure that simply never ends?

JS: Why does the Sibyl want to die? Who could blame her? I also forgot to ask for eternal youth. And look what happened. Just more narrative—in a bad sense.

RB: Sibyl wants to die because she's shrivelled up to the size of a small rodent. Death is not absurd. Old age is.

JS: Hence, the happy resolution to the Achillean dilemma. Better the short, heroic, *kairos*-rich life than slowly wasting away under the auspices of *chronos*. Or, in a modern register, the famous last words of Gabriel in Joyce's "The Dead": "Better pass boldly into that other world, in the full glory of some passion, than fade and wither dismally with age." The problem is that most of us become so accustomed to being more or less pampered pigs that we forget that an heroic initiative still exists. We forget, to quote Tennyson's "Ulysses," that "it's not too late to seek a newer world." Call it the Ithaca Complex. But if one is to remain alive in this absurd world, one should at least have the good (narrative?) sense to make our true Penelope Flaubert. Then we might read the latter's well-known remark to Louise Colet ("What I would like to write is a book about nothing") with a renewed sense of adventure. He later writes to Elisa Schlesinger: "And so I will take back up my poor life, so plain and so tranquil, where phrases are adventures and the only flowers I gather are metaphors."

I conclude: the only "full glory" available to us is in not merely the stewardship of art, but its production. Otherwise, the plain, tranquil life leaves no wake. Flaubert withered dismally. *Madame Bovary* still flowers. No wonder so many artists have been beguiled by the idea of immortalizing themselves by writing. But Keats understood the vanity of that human wish when he insisted that his epitaph read: "Here lies one whose name was writ on water." Good lad. Well-wrought by his Being-towards-death.

RB: An interviewer once asked Woody Allen, "Do you hope to achieve immortality through your art?" To which Allen replied, "No, I hope to achieve immortality by not dying." Unlike Allen, I don't want to live forever, but I understand and appreciate his indifference to "posterity." Shakespeare's thirty-seven plays and 154 sonnets mean as much to the man who penned them as the chop-fallen skull means to Yorick. I like to imagine that Shakespeare derived pleasure—intense pleasure—from writing the words "Shall I compare thee to a summer's day" or "The quality of mercy is not strained" or "Nothing will come of nothing, speak again." But from where he lies moldering in his grave, the *Collected Works* are as important to him as the Telephone Directory of Lower Slovenia is to me. Loam to stop a beer-barrel, clay to keep the wind away. The argument for crafting any kind of life—whether Achillean or Flaubertian—is the happiness one experiences while living it. The rest is silence.

So I ask, why do you care if your life "leaves a wake"? Or if you "immortalize" yourself through art? I want to write my name not in water but in wine. What matters are not the lees that remain after the glass has been emptied, but the fruit that was drunk while the glass was full.

JS: We have nothing to disagree about on this point. The only reason not to hang ourselves immediately is so we can read and write lines as hilariously mordant as "Let's hang ourselves immediately!" I don't know about happiness, but Beckett's wit certainly gives me plenty of disinterested satisfaction. That's just enough—so far—to keep me from the actual rope.

RB: I'm glad to hear you no longer regard literary production as a promissory note to be cashed in the Hereafter. Perhaps I can now also persuade you to abandon the notion that "Absurdity à la Camus is your life blood"?

To me, Camus's philosophy represents a failure of nerve. He no longer believes in the myth of God the Father, but he can't quite bring himself to do without the metaphysical comfort that myth provides. He is, in other words, a reluctant atheist. The death of God has the effect of collapsing Being into Time, thereby killing off Man's eternal soul, a situation Camus regards as "absurd." He allegorizes that absurdity by treating mortality as a Sisyphean burden and then by transforming Sisyphus into an existential hero, a Promethean figure of revolt. But what Camus seems to have forgotten is there are no gods to revolt against. This leads me to three related questions. Why is mortality absurd? Indeed, why is mortality a problem? More to the point, why is it even a matter of concern?

JS: I have no great intellectual love for Camus. When he concludes "One must imagine Sisyphus happy," I am left wondering about his "reasoning." I don't think Sisyphus is at all happy despite his immersion in the existential glory of his task.

My preoccupation with death is not an Absurd labor of love. Death is a matter of concern to me because the prospect of eternal nothingness—while a positive relief in one sense—is not pleasant to consider. What unhinges me more than anything is that there are no sound or suggestive metaphors for death. I came up with one I like because it demolishes a cliché I loathe. So sometimes

I think of death as "the tunnel at the end of the light." My tunnel vision has no philosophical pedigree. Perhaps I was cheering myself up at the beginning of this dialogue in imagining that it does. The fact of death stupefies me. That we can go from quintessence to dust in a single moment is to me the most horrifying thing imaginable. If this still sounds adolescent, then I must admit that I am arrested in adolescence. I am not "sorted" when it comes to the big D, and I suspect I never will be. And reading Heidegger or Tolstoy or Shakespeare won't get me there. So I am depressed. I have been since I was ten years old.

RB: Disease, infirmity, old age—these are the things that unsettle me. Or so I imagine. I suppose it's easy to be philosophical about death, when one is still hail and hardy. You earlier mentioned Achilles choosing *kairos* over *chronos*. No doubt you remember Odysseus' encounter with the shade of Achilles in Book XI of *The Odyssey*. The "Man of Many Turns," the great strategist and talker, attempts to console his departed friend:

> Was there ever a man more blest by fortune
> Than you, Achilles? Can there ever be?
> We ranked you with the immortals in your life,
> We Argives did, and here your power is royal
> Among the dead men's shades. Think, then, Achilles:
> You need not be so pained by death.

To which Achilles bitterly responds:

> Let me hear no smooth talk
> Of death from you, Odysseus, light of councils.
> Better, I say, to break sod as a farm hand
> For some poor country man, on iron rations,
> Than lord it over all the exhausted dead.

It is one of the most extraordinary moments in literature. Better the meanest slave than the noblest hero, as long as one still stands in the light of day. Perhaps it's true that in the end, despite all the "smooth talk," *chronos* casts out *kairos*. Perhaps, when finally confronted with death, we will do anything—betray our friends, betray even ourselves—for just one more breath of life. Is it that sentiment that fills the intensive-care units and the assisted-living facilities? Which is worse? The horror of death? Or the horror of a life not worthy of being lived?

JS: I don't know which is worse: nothingness or a life lived poorly. My fear is the blend: a life lived poorly that ends in nothingness. Perhaps that is one reason I drink. Byron wrote: "Man, being mortal, must get drunk." I know that Baudelaire's winsome "Be drunken continually" is a flowering of that necessary evil, but I prefer Byron's more honest and frankly abject response to our mortal condition. *Chronos* is the death of all *kairos*. I don't see any way of thinking outside that coffin.

RB: Perhaps you know Karel Čapek's play, *The Makropulos Case*, adapted as an opera by Leoš Janáček? It tells the story of certain E.M., a.k.a. Elina Makropulos, Emilia Marty and Ellian MacGregor, who has achieved immortality thanks to a special elixir. When we encounter her she is 342 years-old, but in health and appearance she is a beautiful and vibrant forty year-old. Men vie for her favor and many a heart is broken.

The English philosopher, Bernard Williams, wrote an essay about *The Makropulos Case*, in which he reflected upon the problem of death. For Williams, the play and opera illustrate that "immortality, or a state without death, would be meaningless." He goes on to point out that at the time of the action, E.M.'s "unending life has come to a state of boredom, indifference and coldness. Everything is joyless: 'in the end it is the same,' she says, 'singing and silence.'" She finally refuses to take the elixir again—the plot assumes a dose must be swallowed every 300 years or so—and she dies. Immortality, Čapek, Janáček and Williams argue, would be insupportably tedious.

So I ask: If you could drink E.M.'s elixir of immorality, would you? And if yes, how would you spend eternity?

JS: There's a short story out there (I think by Singer) that ends with a male ghost saying to his female lover-ghost, after having floated about for a while, "Immortality was my greatest disappointment." Is that the converse or obverse of "Let's hang ourselves immediately!"? I understand that death necessarily shapes our every living moment (or should), but my problem is that the shaping is really a crushing, a demolition. It is sometimes so crushing that I want to hang myself immediately. That I have not suggests at once my tenacity and cowardice. Who can adjudicate between these? Not I. Not clearly. I sometimes think that you simply enjoy *life* more than I do. And that enjoyment—because you are so reflexively high-brow—nourishes itself with the headiest of elixirs. If you were a poet, you would be crafting an irregular Pindaric Ode called: "Intimations of Mortality taken from fairly recent Lucubrations in Adulthood."

RB: Although I greatly admire Wordsworth, his sensibility—especially in the "Intimations" ode—stands at a great distance from my own. Like you, he was death-haunted, even death-obsessed. From "We Are Seven" and the Lucy Poems to "Michael," "Intimations of Immortality" and, of course, "Elegiac Stanzas," he may be England's greatest poet of mortality. Oddly, he experienced his own birth as a kind of death and spent his life seeking consolation in memory, time and nature—until the latter killed off his brother and he became inconsolable.

You have lived so much of your life in the belief that Hamlet and Don Juan were your alter-egos. But perhaps the Man Behind the Curtain was really the Bard of Grasmere? Does Wordsworth add anything to our conversation about death? And how close is his graveyard-sensibility to your own?

JS: Not too long ago, I found myself wandering near Windermere along paths that took me to half-finished sheepfolds that had not altered in two-hundred years and more, the straggling ruins that Wordsworth found so worthy of words. What the sad shepherd did not finish building, Wordsworth does, poetic stone by stone, and yet his poems are haunted by loss, even preemptive loss, and not even the most well-wrought poem will earn Wordsworth the right to enjoy the "animal tranquility" he celebrates in "Old Man Traveling." So I think you are right to notice certain similarities. Although I would rather have Byron's *amor fati* coursing (or Corsairing) through my veins, the truth is that I share Wordsworth's fond dread that "Lucy should be dead." The honeymoon of childhood memories does nothing but make me realize how I shall never again lightly draw my breath. When I try to breathe it feels like the opening measures of Mozart's *Requiem*—a labored, painful breathing. From time to time I can enjoy the brio and effervescence of the Overture to *Don Giovanni*, but more often than not I am brought back into the ruined sheepfold of my mortal condition. Few can stare into the Abyss and come away giggling, as Byron and Beckett do—the lucky bastards.

RB: And yet death is precisely the enabling condition of Wordsworth's poetry. The Light—which he sometimes calls Lucy, sometimes Luke—must be lost so that Wordsworth can lift up the stone that Michael will not, thereby transmuting the mute matter of everyday life into the still sad music of humanity. Like the Simple Child of "We Are Seven," the artistic imagination plaits its garlands in the shadow of the graveyard. And isn't that what art has always done? Shklovsky's "defamiliarization" (*ostranenie*) and Brecht's "alienation-effect" (*Verfremdungseffekt*) are about breaking down routine perception, breaking up habits of mind that bleed the color and shape out of life, turning it into a "chronic" condition. In *Critique of Judgment*, Kant argues that the aesthetic is born out of the "free play of imagination and understanding." When we *look* at Monet's painting of a haystack and then *think* about what it represents—the farmer's haystack—we are momentarily disoriented as we attempt to align perception and cognition, to correlate what the mind sees with what it knows. Monet has painted something that both *is* and *is not* a haystack, and as we mentally process the difference—surrendering ourselves to "the free play" of aesthetic sensibility—habitual time, space and perception fall away. In other words, art transforms *chronos* into *kairos*, and it does so precisely by insisting on our temporality. As Walter Pater put it: "art comes to you proposing frankly to give nothing but the highest quality to your moments as they pass, and simply for those moments' sake."

You said earlier that mortality so thoroughly shapes your every moment that you sometimes feel crushed by it. Is it the fact of mortality that weighs upon you? Or the anxiety that your life has become more *chronos* than *kairos*?

JS: Yes—if Homer, underworldly Achilles, Lucy, Luke, Wordsworth and Pater taught us anything it is that *kairos* is our Shepherd. We shall not want. Art [hay]stacks up for us precisely because it seizes its moment. To the extent that I can live inside works of art (I once fell asleep in the painting of Van Gogh's bed), I can tolerate our glass of mortality. But when human voices wake me, I drown in *chronos*. My diseased heart is the graveyard I carry around inside me, but it does little to transmute the mute matter you refer to. And if one cannot be the constant alchemist, then what's the point of going on? The untransmuted life is not worth living. So the good news is the bad news: when I look in the mirror I see Yorick's skull emerging. It usually makes me pour myself another drink. And then look for a painting or a symphony or a metaphor to fall into.

RB: I think we've agreed, contra Camus, that mortality does not make life fundamentally absurd. But neither does it make life fundamentally worthwhile.

You mentioned Nietzsche. I like to imagine that the title of *The Joyful Wisdom* (*Die Fröliche Wissenschaft*) is meant to play off the "Glad Tidings" of the *Gospels*. The realization that the Good, the True and the Beautiful are not given by God or Nature—that values are constructed by humans and are therefore contingent—is for Nietzsche good news, a liberating and exhilarating form of knowledge. Sartre says much the same in his back-of-the-cereal box formulation, "existence precedes essence." Humans are radically free but with that freedom comes the responsibility of choice. And we cannot choose not to choose. There are many different ways of making our lives signify. But if we fail—Nietzsche and Sartre are stern libertarians—then we have only ourselves to blame.

For most of us our lives are works in progress, with high points, low points and a lot in between. That we occasionally see the skull in the mirror should serve to prod us forward, not to plunge us into despair.

JS: I think of all of these dialogues as suicide notes we will have left behind: at once life- and death-sentences, as I said earlier. But the glad tidings are, I suppose, that the Hemlock Society would not have me for a member. And certainly you are not one of them. I don't love my fate or the Yorick beneath my thinning hair, but it's clear that my mortality has chiseled out whatever existential shapeliness I have. And yet I cannot celebrate that fact. I can look upon it with a kind of rueful wistfulness and—I have to say—a certain embarrassment. Better never to have been born at all than face the diurnal round of rocks, stones, trees, students, blue books, exiting wives and the incandescent consciousness that all of this strutting-and-fretting signifies nothing. I have been hanging myself, slowly, since I was ten years old. And it has given me no erection of any kind. So what's the point?

RB: The point to life is whatever you make of it. And if you make nothing of it, then there is no point. My plan: a happy life followed by a quick death. The rest is white noise.

JS: It's not that I make nothing of life. It's that death will make nothing of me. And yet I don't get up at four in the morning just to be—and live—like everyone else. You are the more, I the less cheerful existentialist. You are the Prince of your ambitions. I am Death's pawn. But—as a Persian proverb reminds us—at the end of the game all the pieces go into the same box.

RB: What can I say but … "Checkmate!"

On the Eros of Species

JS: When I think of "love," I think of Nietzsche and the idea that we cannot live without certain illusions, love being near the top of the heap. Nietzsche delighted in lopping off comfortable illusions and beliefs. Most people cannot imagine even trimming their hair.

RB: First you must tell me what you mean by "love." Or—without the ironic varnish—love. Certainly the evolutionary imperative is not an illusion. Indeed it may be the only truth.

JS: How do you imagine that this "imperative" is "love" except in the most metaphorical way?

RB: As Mrs. Moore says in *A Passage to India*, "Love in a cave, love in a church—what's the difference?" Once we brush aside the Arthurian legends and their Hollywood variations, love is essentially the evolutionary imperative to reproduce. Could anything be less "metaphorical"?

JS: Why even call that "love"? It looks like basic instinct to me. Why not just say of "love" what Henry Ford said of "history"? It is bunk. Or perhaps merely a form of lunacy.

RB: Love is neither illusion nor bunk. On the contrary, it is the most powerful and all-encompassing of human emotions. But we find ourselves at a disadvantage, poking and prodding at the flaccid, four-letter word that English provides. Better to turn to the Greeks, who distinguish *erōs* (passionate love) from *agapē* (general

How to cite this book chapter:
Begam, R. and Soderholm, J. 2015. On the Eros of Species. In: Begam, R. and Soderholm, J. *Platonic Occasions: Dialogues on Literature, Art and Culture.* Pp. 95–107. Stockholm: Stockholm University Press. DOI: http://dx.doi.org/10.16993/sup.baa.f. License: CC-BY-NC-ND.

or filial love) from *philia* (friendship). Plato begins to muddy the definitional waters in *Symposium*, when he conflates the philosophical love of beauty with the eroticized love of the body.

Confusion deepens in the Middle Ages with the advent of *amour courtois*, which mixes physical and religious "passions" and produces two of the most benighted figures in all of literary history, Dante and Petrarch. The Florentine poet is a medieval Humbert Humbert, absurdly "falling in love" at the age of nine with a certain Beatrice Portinari, one year his junior. Terrified of the flesh-and-blood woman, he spends his youth swooning over her pubescent image until she finally has the good sense to die at the age twenty-four. This happy event inspires him to develop a revolutionary new poetry (*stil novo*) and later to derive an entire cosmography—not to mention the greatest epic of the period—from the fourteenth-century equivalent of Lolita's mercurochromed knees.

As for Petrarch, he literally takes sublation to new heights—or, depending on your point of view, depths—when he ascends Mt. Ventoux, transforming an amble up a mountain into a transcendent journey of the soul. His vision of earth-shattering beauty comes to him in the form of Laura de Noves, whom he first sees on Good Friday, 1327, and then proceeds to adore from afar, his privates trussed up in lover's knots more elaborate than his own *rime sparse*. Better to have cold, gilded laurels than hot-blooded Laura. In a delicious turn of fate, the lady marries Hugues de Sade, an ancestor of the future Marquis.

In other words, *erōs* is no mere metaphor. It is as real and substantial as the sweaty thighs of an English barmaid or a French coquette. Darwin has a thousand times more to tell us about real love than all the poets who ever sang, suffered or simpered.

JS: So, you want to write a book called *On the Eros of Species*. I am not against the idea. I just don't know what *erōs* really has to do with evolution, unless you see in natural selection the mechanisms of erotic love, rather than the micro-gestures of genetic variation.

Tell me how you would analyze the following episode taken from my always-contingent "erotic life." A few years ago my mother, trying to do a bit of match-making (maternal selection?) told me about a novelist in England called Emma Darwin, who is indeed the great-great-granddaughter of Charles. I did a bit of research and discovered that Emma had recently published a novel entitled *The Mathematics of Love*. It may be that Darwin's (naturally-selected?) scion has a thousand times more to tell us about love than the poets you so diabolically limned and maligned. But my story is not over. Being my mother's scion and heir to her ideas about opportunism ("Nothing ventured, nothing gained," she programmed into me), I ventured out and bought a copy of Darwin's novel and also wrote Miss Darwin an eager e-mail wherein I suggested we might go out for a coffee, I being a fellow-writer and living in Canterbury.

To my delight, she replied and her words stirred a bit of passionate, perhaps even genetically-opportunistic, longing in me. I began to read her novel. After forty-one pages, I found (sexually selected?) only three sentences I liked. I never wrote to Emma again. End of "romance." I rejected her on grounds of aesthetic incompatibility. Is that related to the way animals reject one another because one's peacock-feathers are not as brilliantly colored as another's? If I had courted and married Charles's great-great-granddaughter, would it have been—genetically—a Darwin/win situation for my own progeny and their proclivities for composing prepossessing prose? Is there, as Emma surmised—but, to my dismay, wrote inadequately about—a *mathematics* of love? Is this what her famous forebear was also trying to tell us? And, finally, what does it mean when I "peacock" my prose-style to seduce my readers? Is "metaphor" an exaggerated feature of (literary) morphology designed to attract coy or resistant readers? Does this partly explain the history of love poetry (and indeed all literature) and its often florid, figurative language?

RB: I don't have to write *On the Eros of Species*. It's already been written in the intricate patternings of our DNA that help determine who we are and how we act. What inspires us when we see a beautiful woman ("das Ewige-Weibliche zieht uns hinan") has nothing to do with Plato's conception of Beauty or Dante's vision of Beatrice, and everything to do with what Schopenhauer called Will and Nietzsche called the Dionysian. A less poetic term for this is the "evolutionary imperative," or to speak in more materialist and reductive terms, the reptilian part of the human brain. Of course, contemporary Evolutionary Psychology understands that human beings are subtle and complex animals, who no longer live in caves or beat each other with clubs (except in certain American cities). In the contemporary West—i.e., in advanced and modernized societies—wrestling with words and symbols is more highly prized and more handsomely rewarded than wrestling with saber-toothed tigers. Even within the context of a fairly primitive culture like Mycenae, Homer understands that Odysseus is an evolutionary winner and Achilles is an evolutionary loser. And the rules are pretty simple. Women like winners and men like women. Ergo, the "man of many figures," the man who is *polytropos*, is likely to fare better in the natural selection crap-shoot than the man of *thumos*.

But this is not the entire story. If at bottom it is the evolutionary imperative that drives us, that imperative is not indifferent to the ornaments and refinements of culture. The unfortunate Miss Darwin apparently has a prose style about as attractive as a Galapagos turtle. As Gwendolen says to Jack in *The Importance of Being Earnest*, certain words "produce vibrations" while others do not. Emma's did not. But please note that if "Emma" had been "Edward," you would not have written in the first place. What attracted your interest was not a good prose style or an illustrious ancestor, but a skirt and all that it promised. When it turned out that the skirt, at least as it appeared in print, was dowdy and dull, you took to your heels. Could anything be more classically male? Emma's great-great grandfather would have smiled knowingly and made a note in his journal.

JS: That I skirted her skirt had less to do with her being female than with her undesirable features as a prime-mate, I assure you. Those features kept me even from pushing my prim pawn to square two, the Coffee Date in London. But has evolution evolved? Are you really content to think our mating rituals are programmed by the prerogatives of DNA? The reptilian brain does not court women, even if it does lust after them. Women do like winners but often end up with losers. How do you account for that? And some men—the *erōs* that dare not speak its name?—love men, and thus throw a huge "monkey" wrench into the perpetuation of DNA and the *telos* of the Species.

RB: R-complex, limbic system, neo-cortex. One is reminded of Plato's tripartite division of the soul in *Phaedrus*—black horse, white horse, charioteer. But if the neo-cortex is in the driver's seat, what propels the vehicle forward (Freud's "sex-*drive*") is an ink-colored beast that looks like a cross between Sea-Biscuit and Godzilla. So, yes, it's a combination of nature and culture, of reptilian brain and cerebral hemisphere, but it's the former that gets us off the sofa and on the prowl in the hope that we will land back on the sofa with Zerlina or Donna Anna or Donna Elvira.

Why do some women end up with losers? Because there aren't enough winners to go around. Why do some men end up with men? Because the logic of natural selection is endlessly permuting variety—Lucretius' *clinamen*—and sometimes the "swerve" swerves away from pure functionality. The evolutionary imperative does not hard-wire us to reproduce but to copulate. The logic of the system is massive dissemination, with the understanding that if enough seeds fall, some will grow.

JS: Surely, Zerlina, rather than the other two. She is no Donna, thank heavens. Zerlina at least learns how not to be a shrill harpy, but how to seduce and be seduced, something she displays in her famous duettino with the Don. I love how she extorts kindness and forgiveness from Masetto by asking him to beat her ("Batti, batti o bel Masetto"), which of course he cannot, will not do, once the balm of her voice gentles him.

What men represent to women remains a mystery to me that biology only partly explains. Are women driven by biological imperatives more than men are?

RB: Perhaps Zerlina provides the answer. In "Batti, batti o bel Masetto," she presents herself as the meek and submissive woman ("staro qui come angellina") who surrenders, lamb-like, before the masculine power of Masetto. But her "submission," as he realizes, is nothing more than a pose. The theme of the aria is taken up again in Act II after Masetto, rather than Zerlina, is beaten. She comforts her man in "Vedrai, carino" by offering him the remedy of Nature ("bel rimedio … E naturale"), which she carries within herself as a healing balm ("un certo balsam / che porto addosso"). As she places his hand on her breast, the "batti" of the earlier aria modulates into "Sentilo battere" of the later aria, her beating heart which he now feels. What she offers—and what he cannot resist—is indeed the remedy of Nature, the purchase on eternity that comes with home, hearth and family and that is a thousand times more powerful than Masetto's masculine strength or the Don's masculine vanity.

Nature as *Magna Mater* is the biological imperative that drives women, the healing balm that they alone possess and wield before men as the only possible response to mortality. This is why there is no more comical expression than the "war between the sexes." Women have all the power, men none. It is not a war, but a massacre. As Masetto says after the first aria, "See how the little witch gets round me! We men are weak in the head."

JS: One recalls Dr. Johnson's rueful witticism: "Nature has given women so much power over men that the law, in its wisdom, has given them very little." How perfect that the beating heart lies under the swelling bosom, but which is truly the balm men most desire: that generous heart or the appealing breast that o'ertops it? Ideally, both are presented to us but it strikes me that women enjoy power over men not so much because of the balm of their sentimental and emotional generosity, but because that balm offers a physical pleasure that is so intensely gratifying that men lose all judgment when, as the Don says to Leporello, they "scent femininity." I love the way Robert Browning cleverly depicts that sexual power when he has the pathetic Andrea del Sarto exclaim to his wife, "Your soft hand is a woman of itself / And mine the man's bared breast she curls inside." Although she has nothing but her womanliness to recommend her, Lucrezia enjoys all the power over Andrea, who is merely a second-rate artist. He would seem to have her in the palm of his hand, but in fact she dominates him.

I do think women enjoy power over men to the extent that men 1) fear mortality, 2) desire progeny, 3) want that "balmy" pleasure that women keep both in their hearts and between their legs, or 4) enjoy the chase. As any or all of 1-4 lessen in degree, one becomes less a thrall to Nature and to Women, no? And presumably in later life, these enticements begin to lose their luster. I feel less massacred and weak in the head than I did when I was younger. Is that unnatural of me? Or is it simply, finally, growing the hell up and learning that, in some cases, Artifice trumps Nature, the mind governs the body, and—voilà—*Ecce Cogito*! Or am I just cheering myself up until the next pretty girl flutters into the pub, abolishes my meditations and makes a slavering caveman—or a sonorous Don—out of me?

RB: Do men desire progeny—point two of your four-point erotic program? Perhaps. It is one of the few ways we have of kicking against the pricks of our own mortality. Then again, I'm quite fond of the ending of *Last Tango in Paris*. Do you remember it? Maria Schneider has just shot Marlon Brando. He stumbles out onto a balcony, looks at Paris one last time and then, before falling dead, takes the chewing gum out of his mouth and sticks it under the railing. That's how I want to go. My only progeny, my purchase on eternity—a drying piece of Wrigley's.

JS: I wonder if a way of kicking against those pricks is not so much progeny (although they often result from sex) but rather sexuality, the perfervid embrace of the Younger Female who makes us temporarily—but intensely—forget our aging bodies and desiccating cynicism. Men often chase younger women because they fear death. Progeny, in every sense, comes afterward. I will wait for a reply before I launch a frontal assault on the so-called Weakness of Men in face of the Eternal-Feminine.

RB: What a dreary thought—Age recovering Youth in the arms of Pubescence. Sex, when it's good, is an end in itself. It has nothing to do with providing therapy for—or indulging the nostalgia of—graying Lotharios.

But I suspect that you will now accuse me of inconsistency. Isn't the "evolutionary imperative" a means rather than an end, you will ask. Yes, of course it is. But here we must distinguish between a *species mechanism*, designed to ensure the survival of the group, and an *individual's desires*, which aim simply at achieving pleasure, or more complexly at securing companionship and society alongside pleasure. The sex drive is implanted in us by evolution and its logic is reproductive (i.e., it is means-oriented). But the individual experience of love—genuine love—centers exclusively on our desire for the beloved (i.e., it is ends-oriented), indifferent to auxiliary benefits (the "trophy-bride" who flatters masculine vanity).

If I am right and genuine love is always an end-in-itself, then we find ourselves confronted with a Kantian question, which I will now put. To what extent is love disinterested? Isn't it Augustine who said that when we truly love we desire the good not of ourselves but of the beloved?

JS: Killing Death through Sex is a dreary thought only if it cannot be sustained. Otherwise, it's an enlivening practice, as death-defying as other stimulating sports, like alpine skiing and sky-diving. And what is procreation if not killing death through sex? As for "genuine love," I have no idea what that might mean apart from your brisk deconstruction of it very early in this dialogue. If you now want to add a Saint to the mix, so be it. I am happy to think of love as relatively disinterested, but that love certainly has nothing to do with sexual longing or perpetuating the species. Like Milan Kundera, I think sex and love barely overlap. It is appealing—and Christian—to think of love as focused on the beloved, as a kind of idolatry that also has connections to *caritas*, even to pity. "Love" is a four letter word, obscenely-vague terminologically and dangerously-ambiguous practically. It is a force of Sentiment, where sex is a force of Nature. As for your beloved and, it would seem, ubiquitous Prussian, I must echo a horrid rock star: I Kant get no disinterested satisfaction, even when I am "in love." I am that selfish. And I have plenty of company.

As for the power women enjoy over men, I am not persuaded. Not in the least. Three arguments:

1) Men are physically stronger than women and can sweep them off their feet if they like. That painting with all the Sabine women is not called *The Rape of the Roman Soldiers*. Even sweet and amiable Chaucer, I recall, was accused of abducting a young woman. Men know they can physically overpower women and often do. Some women even like a dominating masculinity.

2) Culturally, men are dominant in every way. From Heraclitus to Hawking, from Giotto to Picasso, from Plato to NATO, men have dominated women in Art, Science, Technology, Politics, Philosophy, Music and Literature. True, women have been denied the opportunities to shine in these fields, but that nevertheless reflects the triumph of patriarchy and the fact that Nature designed women for child-bearing, which historically has meant staying home and taking care of kids.

3) Men who know how to seduce women, can and do with great ease. Women are often far needier than men but they play their one trump card (that precious balm) when men show signs of weakness and attraction to them. So I disagree with Dr. Johnson that Nature has given women so much power over men. Women have as much power over men as men give them in moments of weakness, conciliation, pity and ... love.

Love gentles the man, pitches the woman up on the pedestal, generates sonnets and valentines, cools the blood and denatures the huge superiority men enjoy over women. For better or for worse, it has been and continues to be a man's world. I am not crowing about these facts of biology and history. I am merely reporting them. As Virginia Woolf ruefully observed, addressing herself to women: "You have never made a discovery of any sort of importance. You have never shaken an empire or led an army into battle. The plays of Shakespeare were not written by you, and you have never introduced a barbarous race to the blessings of civilization. What is your excuse?"

RB: What I found dreary was not the idea of killing death through sex (*la grande mort* undone by *la petite mort*), but of aging men chasing younger women to recover their lost youth. Unlike virtue, depravity is its own reward—an end in itself, not a means to something else.

Yes, sex and love are distinct—just as *erōs*, *agapē* and *philia* are distinct. But the whole point of a novel like Kundera's *The Unbearable Lightness of Being* is that sometimes they *do* overlap, which is precisely what happens when Tomas meets Tereza. When these small miracles occur, when the three parts of the brain—the three aspects of the soul—find themselves in improbable and breath-taking alignment, then the earth begins to sing and the heavens to glow. My problem with Dante and Petrarch is not that they discover the spiritual side of love but that they deny the physical side. For them it's all St. Paul and no Song of Solomon. Like an arresting painting, a haunting melody, or a memorable line of poetry, "genuine" love—I use the word with no apology—is a work of art, disinterested in the same way that any aesthetic experience is. We want the thing in itself and for itself. There are no ulterior motives.

As to the "war between the sexes": of course men are physically superior to women; of course men have produced more culture and science than the "weaker" sex; and of course men know how to sweet-talk a young lovely into bed. But, at least in the West, custom gives the final say to the woman. Remember the central joke of *Don Giovanni*. Our hero spends the entire opera chasing after women and never beds a single one. Why? Because they say No. What's a Don to do? Even in *Die Entführung aus dem Serail* (whose setting is, after all, a seraglio!), the Selim declines to take Konstanze by force, even though he has the power to do so. Women decide with whom they shall have sex and on what terms. All the rest is peacock feathers—a lot of strutting and preening before the mirror to distract the puffed-up male from the utter powerlessness of his situation.

JS: Since you have returned to Don Giovanni, I would only suggest that the fact that he enjoys no "conquests" in the opera is to be measured against the hilariously compendious catalogue aria Leporello sings as a tribute to the Don's astonishing success with women. We do not need opera to register the fact that many men have not been at all powerless when it comes to the pursuit of women and sexual consummation. Darwin conjectured, and then proved, that the puffed-up male usually "gets the girl" precisely because he is so handsomely inflated.

When *erōs*, *agapē* and *philia* beautifully fan-tail as a single plumage (*quel panache*!) that is a display of love, I would agree. It is rare. And often it does not survive that horror of conjugal routine called marriage. It seems to me we are dancing around the eroticized version of the philosophical problem of the One and the Many, a problem Aristophanes sketched so brilliantly during his contribution to *Symposium*. We spend a huge part of our lives rolling around in search of the One that completes us. We may settle for the Many, or revel in it, depending on our luck in discovering that the One we truly fancy makes us whole again. That wholeness is, as you suggest, as integrated, lovely, and complex as a work of art. I do not think this love is an illusion, necessarily. But I do think it is not nearly as reliable, trustworthy, or honorable as one might expect. How many times have people fallen in love with the One only to find, years later, after wormwood, betrayal and recrimination, another One to take her place? At a certain point, that narrative starts to look like the Many, does it not? One begins to wonder if one can trust only what Wallace Stevens called "the interior paramour." Can we, finally, fall in love only with our minds and imaginations? Until we drool into senility, they will not betray us or leave us wanting.

RB: You imagine a cool and cruel Don, effortlessly seducing 1003 Spanish señoritas who collapse into girlish vapors and lose all volition at the mere sight of his massive codpiece. I imagine a harassed and beleaguered Don, gamely trying to live up to his reputation as 1003 publicity-crazed women pursue him from boudoir to boudoir. But however we envision our man, at the end of the night the decision to go to bed or not remains a feminine prerogative. Man proposes and Woman disposes—in both senses of the word. If nothing else, I hope we can agree on this: the notion of women as powerless putty in the hands of an irresistible seducer is a Victorian myth, invented no doubt by the well-bustled wives of the period who were fucking their asses off behind their husbands' backs. As for the "puffed up male," I suspect he's a good deal more successful in the animal kingdom than in the human. The female of our species is not stupid. She understands, along with Sainte-Beuve, that "nothing so resembles a swelling as a hollow."

On the question of love as transforming amalgam of *erōs*, *agapē* and *philia*, we agree entirely. And yes, it is rare and, alas, too often fleeting. Does that mean we should become Romantics with a capital R, seeking consolation in our minds and imaginations? I hope not. For that is to go the way of Plato, Dante and

Petrarch; that is to leave the garden of earthly delights and seek a world beyond; that is to forget that nothing in this benighted existence makes life so completely worth living as the warm and welcoming embrace of a woman.

JS: And her hard, gem-like *mind*? Let's not forget that! Oh, for a pub-full of Hannah Arendts and Susan Sontags and Daphne du Mauriers. It is our job to help create such winsome bluestockings, is it not? And do we not most successfully cherish what we (partly) create, as Shaw's *Pygmalion* suggests?

I am left wondering about the Greeks and the observation that they (well, the aristocrats, anyway) glorified the *instinct* rather than the *object* of love. Not being an ancient Greek (high- or low-born), I cannot estimate the justice of that observation. It seems to me the Greeks—that is, the literary and philosophical Greeks—did a bit of both. They turned Love into a Force of Nature and a Force of Culture, and we have been the beneficiaries of that blending for 2500 years and more. But, as you pointed out, their way of discriminating among *erōs*, love and friendship was perhaps excelled by an equal talent for blurring them, as when Alcibiades bursts in at the end of *Symposium* and seizes on the evasive Socrates to both praise and blame him for being so philosophical about love. But even that relatively detached form of love is a thousand times more appealing than the grotesquely-depressive definition of "love" vended to us by Jacques Lacan: "Love is giving something you don't have to someone who doesn't want it." If I believed that, I would curl up and die of despair. If there really is such a thing as love, then it is a lion with satin jaws, a tiger with velvet claws. And we must be forgiven if we endlessly pursue that sweet violence.

RB: As in so many things, the Greeks were right: the *instinct* of love is eternal, the *object* ephemeral. Juliet dies, Cleopatra betrays, Ophelia goes mad, but Aphrodite, Dionysus and Pan haunt the dark wood of *erōs* from the beginning of time to the end. And nothing is likely to vanquish them with the possible exception of Jacques Lacan, who would rather make a diagram of love, complete with mathematical symbols, than make love itself. One begins to fear for the collective psyche of France!

But however eternal it may be, we cannot embrace pure instinct—except as an abstraction. When the black lightning of love falls, it assumes a specific identity: these lapis-colored eyes, that Gioconda smile, this melody of movement and gesture, that honey of flesh and hair. A simple constellation of the senses and we are driven mad with a longing that rushes through us like a tide of life, which is also a tide of death. For it is here that a strange transformation occurs as *erōs* touches *thanatos*. Everything that bound us in time and place, that limited us to the here and now, falls away as we are transported to the rhythmically beating heart of the universe and for one, incandescent moment we cease to be broken and fragmented individuals. We are restored to Earth, to Heaven, to Unity. Until, that is, human voices wake us and we drown.

JS: The Prufrock is in the pudding of love, indeed, but—as you wildly surmise—how quickly (invariably?) does that dessert become desert, the tongue of *erōs* (as we are creating a tropeical paradise, lost) pushed into the groove—and grave—of *thanatos*. Wallace Stevens sent us an epigram: "Death is the Mother of Beauty." Everything is more beautiful because we are doomed. And that goes triple for those intoxicating blue eyes that redemptively fall for us, then fall on others before falling into nothingness, the empty sockets of Yorick. But our DNA is in love with Life and perpetuity. The species will continue To Be, even if our individual loves drown, like Ophelia, in Not To Be.

The Benighted States of America?

RB: I recently came across the following item:

> In the 1920s, a ham producer in Smithfield, Virginia, named Pembroke Decatur 'P. D.' Gwaltney Jr. found a ham in his aging room that, according to his records, had first been cured in 1902. Impressed that it was still perfectly edible, he started taking it with him to county fairs, business conventions, and other events to prove the safety and longevity of Smithfield hams. Gwaltney eventually attached a collar and a leash to the piece of meat and started calling it his pet ham. He even insured it, for $5000. The pet ham soon made it into newspaper articles around the country; in 1932 the syndicated column "Believe It or Not!" ran a cartoon of the ham and its owner alongside a brief caption: "Although never introduced to cold storage, it remains tender and sweet and fit to eat after 30 years." The petrified-looking ham's current resting place? The Isle of Wight County Museum in Virginia.

Gérard de Nerval was reputed to have walked his pet lobster on a leash in the Palais Royal because, as he said, it "doesn't bark and knows the secrets of the sea." I think we can agree that Monsieur Jambon, a.k.a. P. D. Gwaltney, was less elegantly—but more profoundly—mad. When the French are surreal it's called art. When Americans are surreal it's called life.

JS: Forget Gatsby. The Great Gwaltney knew not only how to bring home the bacon but how to take it out for an entrepreneurial stroll. And only an American would imagine eating his household god and pet ham. I don't really know whether to pour animosity or encomia on Monsieur Jambon for his fully-baked, if not richly

---

How to cite this book chapter:
Begam, R. and Soderholm, J. 2015. The Benighted States of America? In: Begam, R. and Soderholm, J. *Platonic Occasions: Dialogues on Literature, Art and Culture*. Pp. 108–122. Stockholm: Stockholm University Press. DOI: http://dx.doi.org/10.16993/sup.baa.g.

cured, ingenuity. I do wonder if people in the Benighted States partly inherited their kooky habits from their British forebears, whose talent for eccentricity is world renown. But perhaps Americans have developed their own way of hamming it up, or rather truffling their madness. But are you really complaining about living in a land where the surreal squeals so happily on a daily basis?

RB: Stephen Dedalus described Ireland as the "old sow that eats its own farrow." Presumably Joyce was imagining a porcine Kronos, having cast himself in the role of an avenging Zeus. And what about the U.S., that over-sized behemoth of waggling and waddling flesh? We have so fetishized consumption in this country that it has become a higher calling, a quasi-religion, our own version of Greek *arête*. We speak of the American consumer in hushed tones of veneration, as though he were a combination of George Washington, Johnny Appleseed and Paul Bunyan. Terms like consumer confidence, consumer spending, consumer safety, consumer protection and consumer price-index are the stuff of White House briefings and Blue Ribbon panels. In the immediate aftermath of 9-11, President Bush said that the most patriotic thing Americans could do was go shopping. In the eighteenth century, Americans served their country by starving at Valley Forge and standing at Yorktown. In the twenty-first century, we max out our credit cards at Best Buy and Walmart.

So, yes, I'm complaining. Complaining that in the U.S. we have made a Hormel ham into the New Messiah. Complaining that what in France is a witty poetic conceit becomes in America a witless sales pitch. Surrealism, as the term literally means, is a way of standing above the vagaries of material reality—not a method for plunging into its venalities.

JS: When I listened to Bush's speech about shopping to restore consumer confidence after 9-11, I was living and teaching in Prague. The next day I went to Charles University and told my students that measuring the vitality of a culture by its ability to feel good about shopping was a sign that America was entering the last phase of its decadence. My bemused students were not impressed. Because their grandparents had been under the heel of first the Germans and then the Soviets, they were trying like hell to forget the past and enjoy the boon of capitalism in all its venal vagaries. Cool stuff was a sign of success and wealth, just as Madison Avenue had hoped. They were not particularly appalled by the materialist tumors growing on their quaint streets in the form of KFC, Burger King and—*horribile dictu*—bars that served Bud Lite (a swill next to which even the most anemic Czech beer is ichor). What I find particularly disgusting is the fact that so many Americans enjoy plenitude yet pretend they are existing in conditions of scarcity, even when the last two generations have mostly wanted for nothing, at least in the middle-class (pagan gods bless Nabokov for calling it the "muddle crass"). Why do so many who have never known want act as if their next Big Mac is their last meal on earth?

So we fiddle with dire prophecies—feckless Cassandras—while Atlanta burns, while America, that still youngish sow, eats its Dixie barbecue, loosens its Bible belt, and waits for a cultural coronary that will spell its doom. To add more fat to this fire, I am ashamed to admit that my adoptive country, Britain, is—as always—following America's lead. Obesity and obedience (the two things your adoptive state of Wisconsin are best at, according to some poll) are the Rosencrantz and Guildenstern of this increasingly sluggish, fatuous, docile country. I still prefer England to the Benighted States, but the infelicitous slurring and blurring of the two cultures give globalization a bad name.

RB: Small "d" democrat that I am, I'm all in favor of giving the *vulgus* what it wants, and then of mocking the *vulgus* for wanting the things it does. So if America—or for that matter the Czech Republic—wants to be a pig in a poke that's fine. But it doesn't mean I won't poke the pig every chance I get.

JS: Speaking disparagingly of the *vulgus*, one is reminded of Nabokov's wistful observation that "There is nothing more exhilarating than philistine vulgarity." Lolita's mother—the fat Haze—epitomizes that vulgarity. She is Emma Bovary without any of the charm or the appealing desperation that makes Emma stuff arsenic into her pretty, torrid mouth. It was you, was it not, who first told me that *Lolita* is "the mind of Europe meeting the underpants of America"? It is indeed a hilarious meeting but even Nabokov said it was not clear who was debauching whom. And, after all, it was the sad clown of Czech literature, Bohumil Hrabal, who called America "The Delighted States." Benighted & Delighted. The eternal dialectic?

RB: You have played the aesthetic trump card earlier than I thought you would. Perhaps out of a sense of dialectical desperation? After all, we have no real disagreement. Culturally speaking, America is one vast consumerist wasteland, stretching from sea to shining sea. True, we have the best museums, orchestras, libraries and universities in the world. But our citizenry couldn't care less. For most Americans, Heaven is one big tailgate party, where the home team wins every game, and the beer and hotdogs never stop flowing. In all of history, there has never been a country so powerful and prosperous that was also so contemptuous of the life of the mind. Even among America's educated classes, there is little or no interest in serious art or music. And books are bought—but not read—by a nation content to have Oprah tell them what constitutes great literature.

And yet out of this swamp of cultural waste strange flowers have blossomed. Henry James and William Faulkner specialized in creating *ex nihilo*, writing sinuous sentences that wrapped themselves around vacuities like a bougainvillea around an invisible trellis. Ezra Pound and T. S. Eliot carried their literary Baedekers across the history and geography of Europe, and then published their travel memoirs as modernist poems. And Wallace Stevens transformed himself from insurance salesman into urbane aesthete, making his uncle into a monocle and discovering comedy in the letter C.

How did these miracles of the imagination occur? America was for its artists what Rouen was for Flaubert. Like the author of *Madame Bovary* and *The Dictionary of Received Ideas*, these Americans made a silken mirth out of a sow's ear, an art of consolation out of a culture of desolation. So perhaps you were right when you saluted the Benighted States as the country where surrealism is to be found in every strip mall. Perhaps we should say, along with Nietzsche, that thus only is America justified—as an aesthetic phenomenon.

JS: Rather, an *anaesthetic* phenomenon, no?

RB: Ah, but it is the patient who is etherized upon a table. Not the poet.

JS: As Socratic gadflies, poking the unfeeling patient into momentary consciousness, we are somewhere between the poet and the pig, I think. And you know what happened to Socrates. He didn't even get published before they killed him.

RB: Unlike the Youth of Athens, the Youth of America are always already corrupted, so we needn't worry about having to drink hemlock or finding a student who will ghost an *Apology* for us. Then again, I wonder what one of our former professors—and no mean philosopher himself—would think of this dialogue. In *Achieving Our Country*, Richard Rorty offers a much more positive view of America than either of us has. If memory serves, you admired the book and were largely in agreement with Rorty.

JS: I remember thinking that Rorty was right about the feckless pretentiousness of the academic Left in our time: that it was shooting blanks to pretend that it had some power in the world of politics. I think you did not admire his smug optimism about America as a Whitman's Sampler of chocolately Songs of Ourselves. Rorty led such a privileged life that he imagined it would be in bad taste to maul the hand that had been so generously feeding him. Many of his tenured, radical colleagues do not have such splendid manners.

RB: Here's one of Rorty's cream-filled bonbons: "Whitman thought that we Americans have the most poetical nature because we are the first thoroughgoing experiment in national self-creation: the first nation-state with nobody but itself to please—not even God. We are the greatest poem because we put ourselves in the place of God: our essence is our existence, and our existence is in the future. Other nations thought of themselves as hymns to the glory of God. We redefine God as our future selves." Care to comment?

JS: What can I say? Those remarks, or confections, are Rorty's version of the American Dream. It worked for him. The experiment was a wild success. He enjoyed being the "God" of the academic world for a few years. He was a great man and a great poem, but when he died it took the press one week to discover he was dead, whereas 10,000 turned out in the streets of Paris when Sartre went from Being to Nothingness. I think most Americans have the least poetical nature, unless the word "poetical" means something as bland and banal as "dreaming up a career that my father did not have." I take it you have an even less sympathetic reaction to Rorty's audacious hope?

RB: It is depressing to see one of the great philosophers of the last fifty years descend into New Age psycho-babble: "We are the greatest poem because we put ourselves in the place of God ... We redefine God as our future selves." Does this remind you of anyone or anything? How about: "We are the ones we've been waiting for. We are the change that we seek." Not having spent the 2008 election in the U.S., you may not recognize the latter as one of Barack Obama's most celebrated utterances (Chicago, 5 February 2008). It turns out that the Song of the American Left is indeed the "Song of Myself."

And yet I think Rorty was onto something in *Achieving Our Country*, something that he himself didn't fully appreciate. His paradigmatic heroes were Walt Whitman and John Dewey. Rorty senses that these are quintessentially American characters, and he's right. Whitman stands for the Egotistical Sublime: all self and no other, all future and no past, all individual and no community. The first hippie, he is the Godmother of the Summer of Love, the Protest Movement and Woodstock, which later becomes Hillary's New Ageism—not to mention her Earth Mother lapel pin. Dewey stands for the Will-to-Truth: whatever we want to believe we may believe because truth is something we invent. The first postmodern, he is the Godfather of Madison Avenue, Hollywood and *Spin City*, which eventually give us Al Gore's "invention" of the Internet and Barack's Blackberry.

Of course, for an earlier America—a pre-1968 America—Whitman and Dewey meant something different. They represented the limitless possibilities of ingenuity and innovation in a country that had freed itself from the past and energetically committed itself to the future. They represented a tough American pragmatism that measured itself in terms of successful outcomes, indifferent to precedent or tradition. These are not bad qualities. Americans have historically been good at solving problems, getting things done, moving forward with dispatch and resolve. But this American grittiness, grounded in a self-interested individualism, epitomizes everything the contemporary Left most abhors about the U.S.

In *Achieving Our Country*, Rorty tries to reconcile an older America with a newer America, but he does not come to terms with the contradictions. The results are most disappointing.

JS: For you, then, it *is* too late to seek a newer America? The "heroic" opportunities represented by both transcendentalism and pragmatism have been squandered or transmogrified into materialist swinishness, at once fat and philistine. What then must we do to bring light to the benighted state of the union? Are we doing it now, in this dialogue, or are we merely kvetching because it is always easier to raze a house than to raise one? Or is it better, finally, to move back into the old, dilapidated but still delighted mansion of *Europa* where the history of ideas is not quite dead until it becomes Islamified into medieval correctness. Then we can talk about the Benighted States of Europe and dream of moving back to the New World.

RB: America will never be the intellectuals' paradise that Thomas Jefferson imagined when he founded his "academical village." In that sense, this is no country for culturally old men. Even urban centers like New York, Chicago and Los Angeles are mausoleums: they offer great museums, orchestras and theatres but it doesn't matter. American life has become so fragmented, anomic and anemic that there is no longer any sense of intellectual or artistic community. Or what little exists is frozen in the amber of cultural institutions, like the American university.

Having said that, I'm a bit (though just a bit) less pessimistic about America's political and economic future. The pre-1968 Whitman and Dewey—the heroic opportunities of transcendentalism and pragmatism—are still alive in this country. To be sure, they are currently in retreat because of the bad economy and the accompanying loss of confidence it has caused. And certainly the current U.S. government is doing everything it can to kill individualism and innovation and replace these values with a bureaucratized and statist model. What will happen in the U.S. over the next few years? I have no idea, but the political choices facing the country are as stark and weighty as they have been since World War II.

As for Rorty, his attempt to reconcile the America of his youth with the America of the twenty-first century is an exercise in nostalgia and wishful thinking. Certainly his efforts were well-motivated if narrowly ideological. But what Rorty would not or could not recognize is that the American Old Left and the American New Left have virtually nothing in common. The former catered to blue-collar workers and focused on lunch-pail issues. The latter caters to college graduates and focuses on life-style issues. I think Allan Bloom understood what happened in 1968 far better than Richard Rorty.

JS: The latest paradox: the open-mindedness that the Left, old or new, ought to champion, has devolved into the closing of the American mind, which is to say the Death of Mind. From the real world of substantive issues and actual poverty to the surreal world (and Unreal Cities?) of intellectual poverty and bankrupting populism. I wonder what Thomas Jefferson would have made of George Bush and Barack Obama. Can you imagine the three of them in the same room together? The same galaxy? In Jefferson, the fledgling States got the leader they deserved. And now? It's no accident that both of us have stayed frozen in the amber of Academe. At least we can still play with Plato, Shakespeare, Byron, Nietzsche, Conrad, Joyce and Derrida as a way of earning our wages. And who knows if we might actually be forging, in our own modest way, the uncreated conscience of today's youth. How? By suggestively corrupting them—that is, making them think.

RB: Jeffersonian Republicanism has much in common with contemporary Libertarianism. Jefferson favored decentralized government, states' rights, low taxes, reduced spending by Congress and a strict interpretation of the Constitution, which he felt was the best way to protect individual liberties. He would have been horrified by Bush's anti-intellectualism, cultural parochialism and Bible-thumping; but he also would have been horrified by Obama's shameless aggrandizement of power to the federal government. I suspect Jefferson would have hated Bush as a boob and feared Obama as an autocrat.

As for our Socratic mission, I'm skeptical that we accomplish much by "corrupting" the youth of America and England. We may affect a few hundred students in our teaching careers. But a few hundred is nothing when you're talking about hundreds of millions of voters. You and I aren't changing the world. We're entertaining ourselves and the (very) few students who are amused by our jokes.

JS: I suspect you are right, hope you are wrong, and tilt toward the nearest pub as soon as I am finished explaining how and why Shakespeare is a mortal god. But do you really care what happens to America and Americans so long as you can draw your paycheck, spend loads of time in Europe and divert yourself by writing books that a tiny handful of cognoscenti will read before they too return to stardust?

RB: I care about America's destiny to the extent that I care about freedom. America has done more to guarantee freedom than any other country in the world in the last 100 years. With mosques popping up in Holland like tulips and Imams running civil courts in England, one wonders how much longer the Enlightenment dream will continue. Perhaps just long enough for you and me to enjoy its benefits before, as you say, we return to stardust.

JS: I read somewhere that there are over 1500 mosques in the U.K. But religion in America is apparently on the rise—again. That rise may be nothing more than increased membership in "the metaphysical club" and therefore decorative and without importance. You claimed at the beginning of this dialogue that consumerism was a quasi-religion. What is more culturally baleful and deleterious: Imams or iPads? Or is this a choice of nightmares? Is America more benighted because it still harbors so many avowed Christians or because the shopping mall is replacing the church as a place of Sunday worship? I think that consumerism registers the slow death of religiosity, and therefore I am not too troubled by it and in fact can welcome it. But there is nothing beyond it, nothing to supersede it, nothing for it to grow into.

RB: I distinguish between Christian fundamentalists who annoy me with their beliefs and Islamic jihadists who try to kill me with their bombs. Of course, the role of religion in contemporary America is a matter of concern. Obviously it is depressing to think that an atheist cannot be elected to high office in this country. Jefferson the Unitarian—the eighteenth-century equivalent of a non-believer—wouldn't even be a viable Presidential candidate today.

IPads or Imams? Without doubt, the former. Radical Islam is fundamentally incompatible with Enlightenment, democracy and modernity—values that we both prize. As for choosing between Christians and consumerism, I suppose it depends. Certainly I would rather spend an evening with T. S. Eliot than with the yahoos who charge into Walmart the day after Thanksgiving, as though they are entering the Holiest of Holies. Contemporary Christians may believe in an illusion but that makes them neither pre-modern terrorists nor postmodern barbarians.

In a sense, what we are talking about ultimately comes down to a debate between tradition and modernity. And at the center of that debate is the issue of levity. What happens when we become thoroughly modern, when we liberate ourselves from religion and society, when we float free of history and tradition? At the end of *The Unbearable Lightness of Being*, Sabina becomes a kitsch artist. Her freedom is translated into empty consumerism. Released from the deadly and deadening gravity of Communism, her identity grows so gossamer-like that it finally dematerializes into a Technicolor puff of air. Something has to ground human beings and all that remains after the Nietzschean transvaluation of all values is aesthetics or the marketplace. And guess which one we choose in the U.S.? Since you cited Wilde earlier, I'll cite him now: "Americans know the price of everything and the value of nothing." Better strip malls and McDonalds than the medieval chamber of horrors that radical Islam represents. But the choice of nightmares is not attractive.

JS: Happily, it does not really come down to that choice for us. America will never return to anything resembling Puritanism. It is too infatuated (note the "fat" larding the word) with Walmart, Victoria's Secret and Burger King (the only Monarch Americans will serve) to allow religious wowsers (as Rorty once called them) to thin out their odious, yahoo voraciousness. I don't see anything all that nefarious happening in Britain as far as the rise of radical Islam, although in some parts of England it is illegal to sell piggy banks because they offend a tiny handful of pious Muslims. The Almighty Pig—like the God it has replaced—often roots in mysterious ways. In both our linked cultures, we may indeed speak of the surrealism of everyday life. But the forces that shaped the two cultures (and the common language that divides them) are still so strong that the reign of the pig is amusing, annoying, but hardly alarming. And as much as I inveigh against the horrors of living in a kitsch culture, there is much to add gravity to the Technicolor puffery.

I am anchored by traditions, especially teaching at a school that was founded in 597 A.D. In 55 and 54 B.C., Caesar marched down the street on which I live. In America, I never felt these weighty traditions, save that charmed decade in the 1980s when we both capered as graduate students at Jefferson's "academical village." I now begin to see why those years were so rich and lovely. We were immersed in history, tradition and ideas, all of them basically rooted in ancient Greek culture.

But the fact that Jefferson himself, at once a Renaissance and Enlightenment creature, could not today be elected President of the U.S. because of his free-thinking is one of the saddest and most disturbing "developments" in recent American history. Jefferson knew the value of everything and the price of nothing, which makes him the opposite of a citizen of the Benighted States. Of course we felt right at home at the University of Virginia, where Jefferson's presiding spirit still haunts those classical colonnades, and where we once strolled, peripatetically, discussing literature and philosophy, wondering how we could keep ourselves from ever having to leave that delighted state of being.

RB: Certainly America is not threatened by a resurgent Puritanism that will turn us into guilt-ridden Arthur Dimmesdales or revenge-seeking Roger Chillingsworths. But our public life is still held hostage by a hypocritical and moralizing Victorianism that occasionally works people and the media into a lather over matters that don't really concern them, as happened several years ago with Tiger Woods, who committed the same crime (heaven forfend!) that earned Hester her scarlet letter.

Of course, once we push through the prim surface of this Victorian posturing, we discover that it's nothing but a shadow-box play. Indeed, in today's America the realm of moral choice has become so medicalized and mediatized—I deliberately use these barbarous neologisms—that *no one* is any longer responsible for *anything* he does. The categorical imperative has been replaced by the therapeutic imperative.

First Porcus is crucified. Then Porcus is resurrected. To revert to our opening conceit, it's a surreal combination of piety and exculpation, a morality play in which the morality is all play, something we invoke so that first we can feel good about ourselves, then bad about ourselves, then good about ourselves. Call it media therapy.

When I spoke earlier of a choice of nightmares, I was invoking two large movements in the contemporary world. The weightless, substanceless, simulacral ethos of postmodern America—all image and no reality—vs. the weighted, freighted and absolutist ethos of radical Islam. Neither is especially attractive, but I'll take bloodless consumerism over bloody hand-chopping any day.

JS: That is a decision that history, ideology and geography have already made for you. You have nothing to endure but the slow, steady decay of tradition, the Fall of the American Empire, the triumph of the Budweiser and brat-obsessed vultures over the well-meaning and meticulous stewards of culture.

In Britain, there is scarcely any difference in that human imbecility and so, from time to time, football maniacs trample one another to death in sports arenas, no matter who is winning the stupid game. I think I am running out of things to loathe about human vice and folly, epitomized perhaps in the excesses and hypocrisy of the United States, but certainly amply in evidence in all Western or Westernized cultures.

The good news is—Porcus the Piggod take me now—also the bad news: we will die before our comfortable and fairly rewarding academic way of life goes the way of the Dodo bird. I reckon our uselessness will be complete in about fifty years when books are obsolete and everyone is either medicated into Neverland or solipsized by advances in virtual reality that will, finally, make us forget the lesson of Plato's allegory of the cave. As Alexander Pope darkly observed nearly 300 years ago, "And universal Darkness buries All" as our benighted grandchildren suffer "the Triumph of Dullness" without having a clue that they are dead souls in a dead world, etherized upon a table but with no poet extant to pound any sense into or out of it.

RB: I hate it when, out of dialectical necessity, I am forced into a position of sunny optimism, or—to speak more accurately—of cloudy ambivalence. Certainly I don't agree with the oft-repeated claim that America is presiding over an empire or that the country's international influence, power and prestige are in *inevitable* decline. Without doubt, we are headed into what the foreign policy experts call a more multipolar world, one in which Europe, Islam, China and India will play different and larger roles than they have in the past. Nevertheless, the U.S. remains the lone superpower in the world, and we continue to produce more scientific knowledge and to generate more wealth than any other country. It is no accident that each year the Nobel prizes almost all come to this country.

The thrust of my argument has been to separate American culture from American political and economic power. To be sure, museums, theatres, orchestras and universities all require wealth, and one of the reasons we have been successful in producing the former is because we have been successful in producing the latter. Where we have largely failed is in sustaining a public intellectual culture, in constructing a forum where our citizenry might see the relations that exist among art, music, literature, philosophy and politics, and then understand how these relations define who we are and what we desire, how they condition our sense of a communal *arête*. Jefferson imagined America as a loose confederation of Greek city-states in which citizen-philosophers would construct a culture founded on the Good and the Beautiful. His ideas were not all that different, *mutatis mutandis*, from the notion of Enlightenment set forth by Kant, whose three Critiques are a coordinated attempt to synthesize Knowledge, Morality and Art. Alas, this utopian vision has not and will not be achieved.

As for your wonderfully Byronic vision of Darkness fifty years hence, I can only say "perhaps." Porcus knows that if the current trend lines continue, legitimate library books will soon be as obsolete as blacksmiths and buggy whips. My one and only hope for the future comes from some of the young people I teach. I sat in a Madison pub until 1:30 this morning drinking and talking with one of my former students about Lawrence Durrell, Marcel Proust, William Faulkner, Vladimir Nabokov, Roberto Bolaño, and the *Iliad* and *Odyssey*. Who says the Platonic symposium is dead? For that matter, that you and I are both generously supported by our respective polities so that we can sit around writing dialogues complaining about those polities suggests that a certain Greek/Enlightenment ideal lives on in the U.S. and the U.K.

The very real benefits we derive from the great Anglo-American tradition of liberalism and tolerance in no sense diminishes the absurdities, vulgarities and stupidities that we have recorded with such relish and delight in these pages. But perhaps your students at Charles University come closer to getting the sometimes Benighted, sometimes Delighted States of America right. Perhaps, to reanimate our favorite metaphor, we whinging academics are the pampered pigs we have been stigmatizing. Perhaps we should be a little more grateful to a culture that enables us to loll about in the mud, even as we build our castles in the sky.

JS: You may recall seeing these words on a daily basis in the 1980s, as we entered Old Cabell Hall, first to take and then to teach lessons: "We are not afraid to follow truth wherever it may lead, nor to tolerate any error so long as reason is left free to combat it." Those are the words of Thomas Jefferson to William Roscoe in 1820, and I remember being proud to be at an institution that was founded by someone so enlightened, courageous and wise. I think certain sad truths about contemporary American decadence and folly have rightly led us to discharge our Swiftian spleen in this dialogue, and I have no regrets about our treatment of the fatuous errors that attend a culture of pampered pigs, even if I am among those swine, or was among them. I am hugely grateful for the time I spent at universities in the States, somewhat sequestered in an academic world where truth, reason and error were words that bristled with meaning. It's the decorative, disgusting "culture" outside the universities that I find so nauseating. There are so few ways of making American citizens at large a bit more intellectual and less obsessed with their mobile phones and automobiles. So I plan to celebrate what deserves celebrating and then whinge and inveigh my way to the grave, recalling Swift's epitaph: "Ubi saeva indignatio / Ulterius cor lacerare nequit."

RB: Swift and Jefferson were both men of the Enlightenment. "Fierce indignation" moved one to write *Gulliver's Travels* and the other to write *The Declaration of Independence*. One chose private irony, the other public solidarity. I think where we have ended suggests neither light nor darkness but twilight, harbinger—who can say?—of dusk or dawn. The U.S. is and always has been the best and worst of everything. There is much to excoriate, much to celebrate. What Whitman said of himself we may say of America. She contradicts herself. She is large. She contains multitudes.

JS: Perhaps you're right. After all, only one-hundred miles on Interstate 64 separates the University of Virginia in Charlottesville and The Isle of Wight County Museum in Smithfield that serves both as show-case and mausoleum for Gwaltney's ominously-pampered pig. In any one of the benighted/delighted states of America, we will encounter vast contradictions between higher learning and eating low on the hog.

PART THREE: PHILOSOPHICAL DIGRESSIONS

The Last of the Cartesians: On Enlightenment and its Discontents

JS: The "father of modern philosophy," Descartes also sired one of the most ridiculous "proofs" of God's existence. Properly to father philosophy is no doubt partly to murder its old connection to medieval theology. So I wonder what kind of Enlightenment maneuver Descartes imagined in that heated closet and how we are still indebted to his breaking away from people who thought God created everything in six days. In his *Meditations*, Descartes offered a new genesis, one that includes God but does not start with God. That he feels compelled to reprise the "ontological proof" of God's existence is perhaps just good manners rather than philosophically compelling. To me, the "proof" has the true scholastic stink to it.

RB: Descartes is retreading Anselm's argument: God must exist because he is perfect and by definition perfection includes existence. It is argument-by-attribution that has the effect of defining God into being. Self-evidently fallacious, it violates Descartes's own Method of systematic doubt, whose first principle is "never to accept anything as true if I did not know clearly that it was so."

Of course, I don't take the "proof" seriously. It is a piece of stage-mummery designed to placate the Church. The case of Galileo's persecution by the Inquisition was still fresh in the memory of Enlightenment Europe. How better for Descartes to protect himself than by constructing a "proof" of God's existence? And how better to demonstrate the imbecility of that proof than by presenting it as a logical absurdity—one invented by the Scholastic tradition (Anselm) that Descartes spent his entire career opposing?

How to cite this book chapter:
Begam, R. and Soderholm, J. 2015. The Last of the Cartesians: On Enlightenment and its Discontents. In: Begam, R. and Soderholm, J. *Platonic Occasions: Dialogues on Literature, Art and Culture*. Pp. 125–141. Stockholm: Stockholm University Press. DOI: http://dx.doi.org/10.16993/sup.baa.h. License: CC-BY-NC-ND.

JS: So you're suggesting his proof is ironically egregious so he could escape the gallows?

RB: Why would one of the subtlest minds in the history of philosophy—and an accomplished rhetorician to boot—construct an argument that any school-boy could refute? Consider Part V of *Discourse on Method*. There Descartes summarizes *The World*, a treatise which he penned between 1629 and 1633 but withheld from publication after he learned of Galileo's condemnation. In the suppressed work, Descartes describes a "new world" that is the exact duplicate of the "real world." He then sets forth "the laws of nature" that govern this "hypothetical" universe, observing that "even if God had created many worlds, there could never be one in which these laws failed to be observed." What is the purport of Descartes's remark? God is constrained by the laws of Nature, but Nature is not constrained by the laws of God—an absolutely heretical position. But notice that our wily philosopher has insulated himself from criticism by the Church. After all, his assertion appears in a work he chose *not* to publish, and it refers to a world that is *not* real but imaginary.

The anti-clerical thrust of the *Discourse* becomes even clearer in Part VI, where Descartes mounts a coded but courageous defense of Galileo. He is careful to say that he does not necessarily accept the heliocentrism advanced in Galileo's *Dialogue Concerning the Two Chief World Systems*, while insisting that there is nothing in Galileo that is "prejudicial either to religion or the state." An extraordinary claim. In effect, Descartes says that one of the central tenets of then contemporary Christianity—God created the World and put it at the center of the Universe—is quite simply wrong and that rejecting this belief is not "prejudicial to religion"! Finally, a few pages further into Part VI, he concludes that *all* knowledge, including that of the "heavens, stars and earth" derives from his Method of reasoned observation, which he has constructed "without thinking of anything other than God alone" ["sans rien considérer, pour cet effet, que Dieu seul"]. In other words, all knowledge flows from Descartes—not from God or the Church—although Descartes is happy to tip his hat to the Almighty for having inspired him.

JS: When Descartes writes that he has constructed this Method "without thinking of anything other than God alone" this certainly sounds as if he has been more than merely inspired, but rather is quite "God-centered" in his methodology.

Otherwise, you make a compelling case. Descartes really did know how to blow the insulation into his writings to avoid telling the truth. Is this what happens when philosophy finds itself under the horrible scrutiny of religion?

RB: Descartes strikes a delicate balance. He makes clear his intentions—for those who have eyes to see—but he needs to do so without offending the authorities. A less circumspect Galileo was threatened with torture and forced to recant publicly. So Descartes constructs a system that not only requires no God but also takes reasoned doubt as its central principle. He then appends as eyewash a laughable proof of God, while burying in the back of his book a defense of the age's most celebrated apostate. To my ear "without thinking of anything other than God alone" is a throw-away—just another sop to the Church.

JS: Who was the age's "most celebrated apostate"? By the way, Harvey, Copernicus, and Galileo were all connected to the University of Padua. Before that, Harvey was a Cambridge man and before that he attended The King's School, Canterbury. I live for coincidences and see them as the only filaments of Providence we can know in a world without God. Did Descartes fool the Church clerics? Why did they not see his proof as laughable?

RB: Surely the Paduan astronomer was the age's most celebrated apostate. In a sense, Descartes didn't have to fool the Church. As long as he wasn't doing damage to ecclesiastical orthodoxy, it didn't matter. As it happens, the *Discourse* was extremely popular, the seventeenth-century equivalent of a best-seller. Descartes deliberately chose to write in the vernacular, and part of the revolutionary quality of the book is that it was addressed to the average, educated citizen rather than clerics and scholars. Not only was Descartes one of the greatest thinkers of the age, but he also laid the foundation for the coming democratization of Europe.

JS: Was Descartes anticipating—and advocating—an enlightened citizenry? That is, was he an early force behind the French Revolution? Was he all that democratic? Isn't the reasoning-mind more of an aristocrat, as Plato understands it, than a democrat? And what about suffering the "tyranny of the majority" over the nobility of resistant ideas?

RB: Descartes does for thought what Luther did for religion. He gets rid of the middle-man. The enlightened individual has direct access to "bon sens" ("common sense" in the seventeenth-century meaning) and therefore anyone can be a philosopher. And if anyone can be a philosopher, then anyone can be a citizen. The *Discourse* is one of the most revolutionary books ever written.

Of course, Descartes had before him the example of the French aristocracy—a pack of pampered, pox-ridden idiots. Which is to say, he had no illusions about good governance coming from the bluebloods. I suspect that he hoped for the kind of democracy envisioned by someone like Jefferson: a group of enlightened individuals who were well-read, well-educated and committed to the general good.

JS: I know we are straying from Descartes's purposively playful (as Kant might say) "proof" of God's existence, but I am intrigued by your observation that "if anyone can be a philosopher then anyone can be a citizen." Could you clarify or amplify the logic here?

RB: Kant is, as you know, one of my other democratic heroes. The three Critiques represent his effort to imagine not only what the enlightened citizen of the future would be but also how to fashion that citizen. That aesthetic education is just as important as moral and logical education is one of the most revolutionary thoughts of all time. Kant is often seen as a latter day Platonist, but the *Critique of Judgment* is as anti-Platonic as it can be.

Kant's "universalism" functions in much the same way that Descartes's "bon sens" does: it is the necessary precondition of an enlightened citizenry in which democracy is available to All.

JS: But are you not assuming a degree of philosophical fluency—if not downright literacy—that few possessed, possess, or will possess, in order to fathom the Critiques, both what they manifest intellectually and what pulses, latently, as democracy?

RB: By constituting the philosophical "subject" as the basis for all knowledge and understanding, and insisting that rational subjectivity is not limited to the Few, Descartes provides a radically new understanding of universality, individuality, enfranchisement—in other words, a new understanding of citizenship. People no longer need to be guided by the State or Church. They are fully autonomous, in a position to guide themselves using the Method. What is more, the ideal of reasoned and skeptical interrogation suggests an entirely new stance with respect to authority. Remember that scholasticism depends on authority (and arguments from it), and it is against scholasticism that Descartes writes the *Discourse*. It was Galileo to whom the Church showed the instruments of torture. But Descartes was far more seditious. And more circumspect.

JS: I do see the Lutheran—and then Miltonic—connection to both, respectively, "the priesthood of the believer" and "the upright heart and pure." I just wonder how slowly, if not imperceptibly, philosophy bleeds its subject-constituting life into the masses who haven't a clue who Descartes is. I smell a Zeitgeist, and a noisy one at that: a polter-Zeitgeist.

RB: Of course you're right. There's the theory of democracy and the reality. As Winston Churchill said, "Democracy is the worst form of government, except for all those other forms that have been tried from time to time."

JS: Churchill also said that the best argument against democracy was five minutes with the average voter.

RB: Churchill probably made his five-minute comment about five minutes after he was voted out of office in 1945.

JS: The planet has been mostly governed, for better or worse, by oligarchies of one stripe or another. I do not think the U.S. is really much of a democracy. I am often reminded that it is a republic. Of course that republic is based on democratic institutions and practices. Could it be that Cartesian "democracy" is one of the tap-roots of modern democracies? How long does it take for a philosophical idea to become a political practice? In ancient Greece, it did not seem to take so very long.

RB: As you know, Athens was a slave-holding society in which 10-15% of the population was enfranchised. It was at best a limited democracy. Yes, Europe and the U.S. are republican in the sense that they have government by representation rather than direct participation of the people. And, yes, they are oligarchic in the sense that it takes a fair amount of money (or appeal to those who have it) to get elected. Western democracy is an imperfect system and a far cry from the more enlightened forms envisioned by Jefferson. Then again, if the alternative is the old Soviet Union or the current Iranian Republic, I certainly prefer Western democracy (in the broad sense of that term). E. M. Forster titled his book, *Two Cheers for Democracy.* Not three, but two.

JS: Byron said he detested all forms of government on the planet and gave a slight advantage to the Turks despite their barbarities. He hated democracy, admired Americans, and gave two speeches in the House of Lords for Liberal causes. He was profoundly bewildered by the vagaries of what we would call "geopolitics" and ended up dying for the Greeks, whom he considered thieves and mercenaries, but who gave him some distant intimation of the ancient Greeks, who represented Periclean glory and whose odd confluence of democracy and slavery sorted well with Byron's peculiar affinities and allegiances. Byron hated *hoi polloi* but also hated canting, smug aristocrats who effectively starved laborers in Nottingham. What are we to make of Byron as an aristocratic liberal, to the manor born, but who also despised the hypocrisy of his Peers and yet at the same time despoiled every poor chambermaid who crossed his path?

RB: Byron's politics were clearly a mess. But his life was a splendid work of art. What to make of the peerless Peer? Better to imitate him than analyze him?

JS: I did imitate him so far that I have written a memoir called *Following Lord Byron*. It is a rueful meditation on the hoary differences between being an academic Byronist and being the Great Man himself. I have given up both analyzing him and imitating him. Byron's clever "proof" for the non-existence of God is worth mentioning: No benevolent God would dream of making his Word so ambiguous and variously interpreted (if not downright contradictory) as to produce a veritable History of Murderous Mischief among various sects and fanatics. Therefore, God—at least a benevolent God—cannot possibly exist.

RB: Let us imagine that God is a Humorist and the World his most amusing joke. What could be more benevolent than to teach man how to laugh? And what better way to do it than by also making him cry?

JS: If, as Oscar Wilde observed, the caveman had known how to laugh, history would be different. But the caveman was too busy eating bloated ticks plucked from Mrs. Neanderthal, avoiding wildebeests and stupidly worshipping the sun for him to develop a sense of humor. How creatures like Plato and Descartes crawled out of caves and turned them into allegories and invented irony almost makes me believe in a divine plan. Actually, that narrative from cave to *cogito*, from insects to irony, from wildebeests to Wilde, really only shows that there is no God but Time.

RB: Irony is the only possible response of any thinking being to *l'homme moyen sensuel*. But that provides no justification for boot-strapping God into existence.

As for Plato's cave and Descartes's oven, they are indeed ironizing gestures, attempts to move beyond a literal understanding of reality. At first blush, they seem to stand at the opposite ends of philosophy: the Ancient and the Modern, the Idealist and the Realist. But in a sense they are the obverse and reverse of the same coin: the invisible world above, the invisible world within. One is the metaphysics of sublation, the other the metaphysics of introspection. But in either case it's metaphysics. I prefer a different philosopher—the Cynic, Diogenes. His tub, a sort of mobile *poêle*, enacts "being-there" some 2500 years before Heidegger, an inside that is also an outside, *Dasein* as street-theatre. And his lantern parodies the Platonic trope of Light-as-Truth, as well as the Cartesian trope of Warmth-as-Presence. He is a tramp, a clown, a performance artist—the Gogo and Didi of ancient Athens. Plato is peripatetic, Diogenes vagrant.

JS: Dialogue as dialectic is itself a vagrant—"extravagant" if you like etymology, and I do. The language game which passes the time (rather more quickly than other im/postures) swerves Lucretiously and ludically all the moon long to keep us from fear in a handful of quintessential stardust. Irony: either the devil's mark or the snorkel of sanity (my true Penelope is Flaubert's Parrot).

I know we have already discussed Death, but let me append a quick footnote. One of the things that so terrifies me about the End is the implosion of the possibility of dialogue—the "I could not see to see" (Emily Dickinson) transposed from sight to saying, the way of saying, the mouth (W. H. Auden) shut and full-stopped. That's why I cannot imagine not being, to your Didi, a Gogo dancer in the dark theatre of cyberspace, with fingers at the tips of my words, wheeling out Descartes before Horace, matutinally and nocturnally, as the hands wander across the keyboard with a kind of peripatetic vagrancy, to the last syllable of retarded time, telling tales of idiosyncrasy, signifying—however ironically—something, until Gogo becomes Gonegone. Arrest is silence.

RB: Ah, but Diogenes was not a dialectician. He was a one-man theatrical troupe, a side-walk vaudevillian, a lie-down comic, talking, eating, sleeping in his *pithos*—precursor of Beckett's urn. For him "vagrancy" was monological because in all of ancient Athens—hunt though he did with lantern in hand—he could not find a worthy interlocutor. Plato and Aristotle were the well-heeled academics of their time, and even Socrates was enough of an establishment-figure that the citizens of Athens finally decided to cancel his tenure.

You say that what terrifies you about death is the implosion of dialogue. Quite right. Beckett's "long sonata of the dead"—as he called the Trilogy—is the fullest exploration we have of the monologue as form. It is solitary and self-enclosed, Descartes rewritten as Being-towards-death. But Beckett's sonata is not the end of language games but a reimagining of all their previous possibilities. For Shakespeare, the greatest dialogist of all time, when the stage empties the rest is silence. Even his most brilliant monologist—*il se promène lisant au livre de lui-même*—requires an audience. But part of Diogenes' brilliance is the possibility that it is not a performance. Or if it is, that he is his own one-man audience. When Alexander the Great hears of Diogenes he pays a visit, asking if there is anything he can do for the philosopher. "Yes," comes the reply, "get out of my light!"—an utterance that at once rebuffs a King and reimagines the Parable of the Cave.

Socrates was the gad-fly of Athens. The sting of dialectics produced vision. Emily Dickinson's buzz-fly produces blindness. Death cuts off light. And yet imagining that process becomes its own language game—poignantly monological in Dickinson's case—which produces its own insight. So too with Ivan Ilyich being pulled into his black bag. The conversation of self with self releases language and re-leases it in the sense of renewing it. But we must not forget the counter-example Flaubert provides in "A Simple Heart": Felicité, for whom death comes not as a buzzing fly but as a cosmic parrot. In the end, the parrot Loulou—whom we last saw in a state of taxidermic decay—is reborn as the Holy Ghost, hovering over the entire arc of Felicité's life. For Flaubert, people are as stupid in death as they are in life. I suspect dear old Diogenes would have agreed. After all—as one of your students once said, mangling the cliché—"it's a doggy-dog world." And I'm sure I needn't remind you of the etymology of "cynic."

JS: Cynics are snarling dogs but Jack London, for whom the canine of the species was the Überhund, profoundly disagrees as he makes DOG the inverted or reversed/cancelled/preserved GOD, a distinctly American *Aufhebung* that out-eagles Hegel. On this reading, America is the opposite of Cynicism, a brute blood that defies Doubt and makes a nation out of sturdy vitality. Until recently, that is. But let me pick up on one strand of the luxuriance you uncoiled in my direction.

"When the stage empties the rest is silence." The best thing ever written about Shakespeare is a brief parable by Jorge Luis Borges, "Everything and Nothing." It combines Renaissance self-fashioning, egoistic elasticity, Hamlet's deft/daft theatricality, Descartes's heated constitution of the subject and the implosion of the ego when it no longer can language-forth or stage itself. Here's the ending of Borges's short piece:

> For twenty years [Shakespeare] persisted in that controlled hallucination, but one morning he was suddenly gripped by the tedium and the terror of being so many kings who die by the sword and so many suffering lovers who converge, diverge and melodiously expire. That very day he arranged to sell his theatre. Within a week he had returned to his native village, where he recovered the trees and rivers of his childhood and did not relate them to the others his muse had celebrated, illustrious with mythological allusions and Latin terms.
>
> He had to be "someone": he was a retired impresario who had made his fortune and concerned himself with loans, lawsuits and petty usury. It was in this character that he dictated the arid will and testament known to us, from which he deliberately excluded all traces of pathos or literature …
>
> History adds that before or after dying he found himself in the presence of God and told Him: "I who have been so many men in vain want to be one and myself." The voice of the Lord answered from a whirlwind: "Neither am I anyone; I have dreamt the world as you dreamt your work, my Shakespeare, and among the forms in my dream are you, who like myself are many and no one."

Not to be "staged" is to be pulled into a black bag without redemption. Did this insight occur long before Shakespeare, as *mythos* and *logos* vied for supremacy in the *polis*? The Platonic dialogue, as Nietzsche observed, floated as a life-raft from the wreckage of early Greek tragedy. Plato's Socrates, trying to outmatch Homer's often wind-baggy Odysseus, holds forth (stand and verbally unfold yourself), a male Scheherazade singing for his moussaka, talking himself both out of and into his grave. Language has been a game from the very beginning, I suspect, and it is the most profoundly important game insofar as it keeps us swerving away from Death. Not to have forked (a double swerve) a bit of lightning before dying is the best reason to rage against the dying of the light. And what is a proper dialogue but light/ning forked? And what is the serpent's tongue but beguiling duplicity, a fork in language—beautiful lies? Satan, that rhetorically diabolical liar/lyre.

RB: Wild dogs and Englishmen: Diogenes, London, Shakespeare. Borges's parable is one of the best glosses of the Bard. And certainly the boy from Stratford understood the One and the Many as well as the author of *Parmenides*. But is literature merely or principally a form of consolation, a way to swerve, fork, beguile away the darkness? Since we have drifted back onto the topic of Death, let us return to Camus, whom I abused—perhaps unfairly?—in an earlier dialogue. If for Descartes the central question of philosophy is Being ("How do I know that I am?"), for Camus it is the possibility of Not-Being ("Why should I continue to exist?"). As he writes in *The Myth of Sisyphus*, "There is but one truly serious philosophical problem, and that is suicide. Judging whether life is or is not worth living amounts to answering the fundamental question of philosophy. All the rest ... comes afterwards." Not the rest is silence, but the rest comes afterwards. The Melancholy Dane speaks of the "undiscovered country, from whose bourn / No traveler returns," while the Melancholy Frenchman opens his meditation on suicide with Pindar's "O my soul, do not aspire to immortal life, but exhaust the limits of the possible." Is the limit or bourn of Being a form of Not-Being? Has Descartes constructed his *poêle* with spades and mattocks on the wormy soil of a Danish graveyard?

JS: I want to keep Descartes steadily in our sights to see in what sense we are or might be the last of the Cartesians. Is there a way to hold all this together: Descartes's heated closet as incubator for the *cogito*, the prominence of doubt in his scheme, the question of suicide as prior to all philosophical concerns, and the eruption of self-consciousness in Shakespeare and his greatest puppet, Hamlet? Let us think of Ophelia as the glue-gun (perhaps held to her head) that might make all the above adhere in some peculiar way.

How odd and lovely that, just forty years before Descartes makes Doubt the centerpiece of Modern Philosophy, Hamlet writes the following in his billet-doux to Ophelia.

> Doubt that the stars are fire
> Doubt that the sun doth move
> Doubt truth to be a liar
> But never doubt my love …

Hamlet knows that this "love lyric" is shamelessly anaphoric doggerel, and he gives it up in favor of a simple, prosaic confession of his affection. But insisting that Ophelia must doubt everything around her except Hamlet's love may be a kind of literary premonition—or report—of the centrality of doubt in the Renaissance mind, perhaps anticipated by Montaigne and far more distantly—if whimsically—by your friend, Diogenes. Doubt that the sun doth move? A Galilean doubt? Ophelia does end up having to doubt everything, including Hamlet's love, at the end of the nunnery scene and, after drowning (herself?) in the river, we hear at her funeral from the "churlish priest" that Ophelia's "[d]eath was doubtful." Indeed. Or was it rather a triumph of the will to negation? A Schopenhauerian work of art? In *The Myth of Sisyphus*, Camus writes of suicide (I quote from blighted memory): "An act like this is a masterpiece and is prepared for in the long silences of the human heart." Ophelia did not have much time to prepare—"The readiness is all"—but her "suicide," as the Pre-Raphaelites intuited, was the stuff of art, and Lizzy Siddal actually died shortly after "sitting" (lying in a tub of cold water) for the most beautiful painting we have of Ophelia drifting to her muddy death. Life imitates Art unto [Floating-towards-] Death.

RB: Hamlet's dubious valentine is odd and lovely indeed! If for Descartes self-knowledge is the only certainty in a universe of doubt, then for Hamlet the only certainty is love. Not *cogito ergo sum* but *amo ergo sum*. And can we read his letter to Ophelia as an oblique response to Polonius's "to thine own self be true," a decidedly Cartesian pronouncement that also relies on an astronomical metaphor ("it must follow as the night the day")? Pushing matters further, might we argue that such a reading parodically anticipates Descartes, reducing him, *avant la lettre*, to a pinch-penny of the intellect, an accountant of consciousness whose apodictic philosophy makes the world safe for certainty? Polonius—prudent, circumspect, finical—is Descartes by other means, Descartes as the father of risk-management.

But obviously this is only part of the story. For if Polonius fears that the cosmopolitan center will undo Laertes, the intellectual center has already undone Hamlet. The young prince has been unfitted for rule, made soft and indecisive, too Christian ("never doubt my love") for the half-pagan country of his birth. This, of course, carries us into Paul Cantor's reading, which recognizes that in a real sense the central problem of the play is to be found in its form. The defining ethos of the "revenge tragedy" is pagan, but Shakespeare writes for an audience that is Christian. In other words, *Hamlet* provides us with a Hegelian tragedy that dramatizes the conflict between two equally valid world views: the Machiavellian and the Pauline. We have good reason to believe that Shakespeare read *The Prince*, and no work better articulates the *Realpolitik* of pagan Rome and semi-pagan Denmark. Moreover, such an interpretation gives added meaning to Hamlet's revulsion at Gertrude and Claudius's betrayal of his father, which is after all a betrayal of both connubial and fraternal love. If the new philosophy that Hamlet has learned at Wittenberg is predicated upon love, then what is such a fellow to do, "crawling between earth and heaven"—between paganism and Christianity?

But matters are more complicated still. Shakespeare was introduced to the Continental strain of skepticism by his reading of Montaigne's *Apology for Raymond Sebond*, the central question of which is "What do I know?" ["Que sais-je?"]. Certainly Descartes had Montaigne's famous essay in mind when he wrote the *Discourse*. Perhaps Shakespeare's dialectic is a trilectic, a play that measures St. Paul against Machiavelli against Montaigne: love vs. power vs. doubt? Is Ophelia the "floating" signifier of all three, the broken blossom whose love is destroyed by power and whose doubt becomes so radical that she finally ceases to be? Is she the Cartesian *poêle* reimagined as a Romantic, flower-bedecked bower, drifting down a stream of skeptical, all-too-skeptical, consciousness? In her last scene, Ophelia's weak arms (counterpoint to Fortinbras) are filled with the flowers not of evil but of doubt and disillusionment—a doubt and disillusionment that derive, as you have pointed out, from thought (her pansies are *pensées*). Caught between three world systems, Ophelia's end might be glossed as a rewriting of Descartes: not "Je pense, donc je suis," but "Je pense, donc je péris."

JS: The first thing that occurs to me is the Rortyean suggestion that philosophy is or should be a sub-genre of literature. Or that it always has been, from Thales' monistic intuition (no reasoned *logos*) that "all is water" to Heidegger's *alētheia*. So of course there is something merely academic and always already belated about Descartes's immensely academic "accounting" of and for consciousness. Hamlet's "meditations" on the centrality of consciousness ("There is nothing either good or bad but thinking makes it so") incubate a sovereign *cogito* that anticipates Descartes's impressively doubting *res cogitans* and usurps Claudius's drearily-political—and murderously-achieved—status as king (Hamlet says, "The king is a thing—of nothing"). As for Ophelia's thoughtful sadness, I am reminded of Byron's Manfred, who tells us that "Sorrow is knowledge. The tree of knowledge is not the tree of life." I suspect Enlightenment thinkers would disagree. But the gloomy, stormy Romantics liked to reprise Hamlet's (and Ophelia's) voluptuous melancholy and see too much knowledge as a kind of poisoning of the soul.

And that brings us to Nietzsche's late-Romantic reading of Hamlet: "Knowledge kills action." Too much thinking sinks us every time, sinks us to *gravitas*. "Art comes," Nietzsche observes, "as a saving sorceress, expert at healing," and thus levity, staged as linguistic prowess, ingenuity and dialectical pyrotechnics, comes out of the closet and teaches the caveman how to laugh or, in the case of Byron's Italian masterpiece, *Don Juan*, how "to giggle and make giggle." The specific gravity of intellection is converted to a book of laughter and forgetting that pulls us out of the mud and muck to discover buoyant Beckett waiting for us, his funeral baked meats furnishing forth the gaming tables of drama, where "nothing" happens once, twice, thrice, or as often as necessary to keep the language game going. As we are perhaps "currently" demonstrating, as a "riverrun/s" through us?

RB: Your synoptic view carries us—speaking of *Finnegans Wake*—full circle. In Shakespeare, skepticism produces tragedy (the death of Hamlet), as the authentic individual is achieved, but at the price of his life. In Descartes, skepticism produces comedy (the birth of the Enlightenment), as the reasoning individual is achieved, but at the price of his alienation from self and world. For Byron and Beckett skepticism leads neither to tragedy nor comedy but to irony. Their levity, like Nietzsche's, consists in playing with gravity. For them the only constant is contingency. "Darkness" may be the first poem ever written about entropy, the heat-death of the universe. Small wonder that Byron is the presiding absence-as-presence in *Arcadia*, Tom Stoppard's play about fractal mathematics, chaos theory and the second law of thermodynamics. Or that one of the characters actually quotes a stanza from "Darkness" toward the end of the play. Or that—let us now close the circle—Descartes's heated closet effectively froze when it encountered the snowy wastes of Scandinavia. The Method we are told was born out of a dream. Did Descartes foresee his own end when he invented the Enlightenment in a moment of fitful sleep? Here is how Byron puts the matter:

> I had a dream which was not all a dream.
> The bright sun was extinguished, and the stars
> Did wander darkling in the eternal space,
> Rayless, and pathless, and the icy earth
> Swung blind and blackening in the moonless air …

JS: Halfway between Hamlet's meditations and Descartes's *Meditations* is the latter's famous dream on the night of November 10, 1619, the vigil of the Feast of St. Martin of Tours, which was a time of great feasting in France. Here is how one commentator puts it:

> Having in mind, for a number of years, a project and method to bring all the sciences together within the context of a new universal philosophical "wisdom," Descartes interpreted the vivid

> dreams that he had on the night of the Vigil of the Feast of St. Martin as a sign from God Himself. From that moment on, Descartes would believe that he had a divine mandate to establish an all-encompassing science of human wisdom. He himself was so convinced of this divine endorsement of his "mission," that he would make a pilgrimage to the Holy House of Loreto in thanksgiving for this "favor."

We have indeed come full circle to Descartes's ontological proof of God, which seems to have had a biographical, if dreamy, origin in 1619. This is a dream of Enlightenment, even Pauline epiphany, that may be "comic" in form, as you suggest, but Byron's "Darkness" does seem light-years away from a God-haunted dream. I love Byron's poem as a premonition of both a post-nuclear wasteland and the heat-death of the universe. Both visions are close to my heart of darkness and my fond daydream of a universe that either bears no trace of humanity, or that has disordered itself into a state of perfect chaos where the last Cartesian persists only as a stardust memory.

RB: Descartes's dream is justifiably famous, but whether he actually believed it was inspired by God, merely claimed it to be, or invented the whole damned thing is something we cannot know. Still, I take your larger point: how fitting that the Dream of the Enlightenment was itself the product of a dream, one that was predicated at least in part—and whether as a matter of political expediency or existential belief—on the dream of God. Stardust is indeed a form of memory. By the time the light reaches us the star may itself be extinguished. We might say the same of culture. Each new layer inevitably rests on what came before, which means that the past must settle gradually under our feet before we can walk into the future.

I suspect that Descartes knew that God could not be thought away in a single night. So too with the Enlightenment humanism Descartes gave us in the place of religion. It is only in the last century that we have come to realize that the *cogito*—not to mention the rickety *poêle* that houses it—is just as much a Castle in Spain as that ampler piece of real estate, the City of God. The stars communicate, but over vast distances of space and time. It took almost 350 years after the *Discourse on Method* before we had Nietzsche, a philosopher who decisively undermined our belief not only in God but also in Man. Is it any surprise that the First of the Non-Cartesians was a Greek by temperament, if not by birth?

JS: "Man is a bridge," hoped Nietzsche. A bridge leading beyond good and evil, a post-Enlightenment bridge, for most a bridge too far. Indeed one wonders if *hoi polloi* have ever crawled out of the darkness long enough to see not only that God does not exist, but that "Man"—like the *cogito*—is an unsatisfying fiction.

Nietzsche's Cow: On Memory and Forgetting

JS: The person who makes a shopping list is not the same person who reads it later. I find that intriguing and vaguely disturbing—but also liberating.

RB: Forgotten shopping lists, forgotten umbrellas, forgotten selves. Being-in-time. It is the paradigm for modernism. We discard the past so that we may create the future. Joyce memorably states the case in *Ulysses*: "As we weave and unweave our bodies from day to day, their molecules shuttled to and fro, so does the artist weave and unweave his image." And yet, our archetypal modernist—the man who read everything and forgot nothing—adds the following: "through the ghost of the unquiet father the image of the unliving son looks forth … So in the future, the sister of the past, I may see myself as I sit here now but by reflection from that which then I shall be."

JS: Does any great artist ever discard anything? It seems to me that, because nothing is lost on an artist, nothing ever is forgotten. The meanest memory that flowers often gives thoughts too deep for tears, to amend Wordsworth, that Übermemorymensch. *Ulysses* and *The Waste Land* are deeply memorial texts. The opposite of mad Ophelia is ominously sane Eliot, who can connect anything with anything precisely because his mind is a cultural echo-chamber—that is, memory's sonorous mausoleum. Why even speak of forgetting if this is the achievement of memory? One is tempted to construct a slippery sliding scale of memory/forgetting, with shopping lists at one end and *Ulysses* at the other.

How to cite this book chapter:
Begam, R. and Soderholm, J. 2015. Nietzsche's Cow: On Memory and Forgetting. In: Begam, R. and Soderholm, J. *Platonic Occasions: Dialogues on Literature, Art and Culture*. Pp. 142–158. Stockholm: Stockholm University Press. DOI: http://dx.doi.org/10.16993/sup.baa.i.

RB: And yet Eliot, having suffered a mental breakdown, shores up his own ruined identity with a series of fragmented memories. You call him ominously sane, but he compares himself to mad Hieronymo, Kyd's counterpart to Ophelia. Remember what Eliot says in "Tradition and the Individual Talent": for the modern writer the entire history of literature "composes a simultaneous order." Isn't the inability to forget—to distinguish between the antecedent and the contemporary—a form of madness? To be modern is to absorb the past so completely that it becomes the present; but it is also to break with the present so completely that one risks breaking with one's self. Is modernism just another word for schizophrenia?

JS: Let me respond with a query. What did it mean when Stephen Dedalus said, "History is a nightmare from which I am trying to awake"? What does that nightmare consist of and what has our memory/forgetting dialectic to do with it?

RB: For Eliot the present is mad. For Joyce the past is a nightmare. Best to forget both?

JS: I take it that Nietzsche's cheerful "God is Dead" was an attempt to actively forget (*aktive Vergesslichkeit*) both his dismal present and all the values and beliefs associated with Judeo-Christianity and Western metaphysics. Perhaps much of the vitality of modern art emerges from that murdering of present and past values and traditions, and yet one must know the traditions thoroughly in order to transmute, transvalue and transcend them. How one can actively forget—Nietzsche called that ability "a *positive* faculty of repression"—is a mystery. Emerson called it "self-reliance" in his essay by that name. But it would seem that only those who are deeply steeped in the past create anything worthwhile in the very attempt to forget it. That's why "April is the cruellest month" mixing memory and desire, at once nodding to Chaucer's famous opening in the "General Prologue" and pushing far beyond it. I wonder if the shallowness of so much contemporary art—not to mention the superficiality of so many human beings—results from having almost no literary, philosophical or historical memory.

RB: There are two ways to be contemporary: consciously and unconsciously. The first we call modernism, the second solipsism. One is reminded of Nietzsche's happy cow from the Second of the *Untimely Meditations*. It forgets nothing because it remembers nothing. Each mouthful of grass is as delicious as the last. And it is struck with wonder and admiration at every one of its evacuations, as though it had just produced the *Mona Lisa* from its hindquarters.

JS: Those cows have been pasturing in my imagination for decades. What is remarkable is how closely human beings can be herd-like in their capacity for passive forgetting and the form of solipsism you mention. I suppose I have always looked to art for solace and succour because it represents the opposite of the oblivious cow. But it is difficult to avoid the nightmare of history unless one is an artist or a highly-artistic interpreter, with all the madness those roles may entail. Better to be a lunatic than a happy cow? And yet I thought our Zen-masters taught us to live in the present.

RB: Our Zen-masters teach us to welcome both the nightmare and the madness. Without them we cannot be truly modern. No doubt you recall the beginning of Joyce's *Portrait*: "Once upon a time and a very good time it was there was a moo-cow coming down along the road ..." It is an exercise in modernist forgetting and remembering, in making the new out of the old.

The most ancient of story-telling formulas is transformed into something modern when we realize that Joyce has placed it in ironic quotation marks. And what about our four-legged friend, the little moo-cow? I like to think she has wandered in from Nietzsche's Second *Meditation*, a reminder that to be modern is necessarily to be out of joint with one's time, at once *unzeitgemäss* and *unzeitig*.

JS: I am inescapably (not that I have any wish to escape) reminded of Hamlet's last lines in Act 1, scene 5, when, having just seen his unquiet ghost-father and realized the horrible revenge he must pursue, he remarks: "The time is out of joint. / O cursèd spite that ever I was born to set it right."

Is Hamlet the first modernist? Two scenes later he will say, in his first soliloquy, "Heaven and earth—must I remember?"

Hamlet the Malcontent, driven to lunacy—both premeditated and unpremeditated—an unliving son looking forth at the duty to kill Claudius and wishing he had never been born, already plumping for "not to be." No wonder that Shakespeare's play is remembered in *Ulysses* more than any other text, including *The Odyssey*.

RB: Both Hamlet and Stephen are history-haunted, the one by the ghost of the father, the other by the ghost of the mother. But these characters stand in strikingly different relations to their pasts. Hamlet is the defender of tradition. For him the time is out of joint not because it lacks a natural order, but because that natural order has been violated by Claudius and Gertrude. Although Hamlet is not temperamentally suited for the task before him ("O cursèd spite"), he knows what it is and dedicates himself to achieving it.

Stephen also bears the burden of an oppressive historical memory: the violation and subjugation of Mother Ireland. But unlike Hamlet, Stephen has no desire to restore his ancestral patrimony, turning away in disgust from both Irish nationalism and English imperialism. The model he takes for himself is not Hamlet but Shakespeare; hence, his "theory" of *Hamlet* in which Stephen "proves by algebra" that Shakespeare "is the ghost of his own father."

What could be more modern than to become one's own precursor? The most radical of Harold Bloom's revisionary ratios is *apophrades*: the dead return but as *imitations* of the living. Hamlet avenges the ghost of the past; Joyce becomes that ghost.

JS: Harold Bloom blooms an *Apophrades Complex*. Shall I number those streaks? Hamlet's problem (from Coleridge to the present) is that he has no desire to be Prince and restore anything patrimonial. He is far too matri-*moanial* to re-mind himself of his Conventional Revenge. By Act 5, scene 2, he has (as our students would say) "like totally forgotten his dead dad" and the imperatives that would Spanish-tragedy him (has "Spanish-tragedy" ever drawn its blade as a verb?) into "to be." Revenge is the mother of compression. All of these abstruse musings dally in the most efficient memory-and-forgetting line ever penned by that mortal god from Stratford: "Thrift, thrift, Horatio—the funeral baked meats / Did coldly furnish forth the marriage table."

RB: By Act 5, scene 2 Hamlet has "totally forgotten his dead dad" and the "imperatives" of revenge tragedy? Then please explain the following:

HORATIO:
So Guildenstern and Rosencrantz go to't.
HAMLET:
They are not near my conscience; their defeat
Does by their own insinuation grow.
'Tis dangerous when the baser nature comes
Between the pass and fell incensèd points
Of mighty opposites.
HORATIO:
Why, what a king is this!
HAMLET:
Does it not, think thee, stand me now upon—
He that hath killed my king and whored my mother,
Popped in between th' election and my hopes,
Thrown out his angle for my proper life,
And with such coz'nage—is it not perfect conscience? (V.ii.56–66)

Hamlet is bent on bloody revenge ("Between the pass and fell incensèd points / Of mighty opposites), a revenge inspired by the memory of a betrayed and murdered father ("He that hath killed my king and whored my mother").

Hamlet is modern in his psychology, but not in his time-consciousness. He doesn't want to overcome the past. He wants to restore its lost order.

JS: A palpable hit. But Johnson was right to see that the catastrophe in Act 5 is not felicitously brought about. It is nearly a *deus ex machina*. Hamlet does not avenge his father's death. He avenges his own, and perhaps his mother's. And he seems steeped in Christian resignation ("There's a divinity that shapes our ends") after he returns to Denmark. Hamlet is the ultimate puzzle when it comes to the memory-forgetting dynamic. That he was born to put time into its joint is a cursed fact for him. And he knows that no matter what he does, he will end up like Alexander and Caesar: clay stopping up a beer barrel. Yorick is both his past and his future, all of our futures.

RB: This is the same Samuel Johnson who preferred the revised version of *King Lear* in which Cordelia comes back to life at the end? I myself think the catastrophe is masterfully wrought and that Shakespeare makes perfectly clear that Hamlet has—however belatedly—avenged his father:

HAMLET:
The point envenomed too?
Then venom, to thy work …
Here, thou incestuous, murd'rous, damnèd Dane,
Drink off this potion. Is thy union here?
Follow my mother. [*King dies*]

LAERTES:
He is justly served. (V.ii.304–5; 308–10)

Hamlet, as we discussed in another dialogue, is caught between two worlds—one Pagan, one Christian. What he has learned at Wittenberg, where he would have studied theology and philosophy, has made him a good scholar but a bad prince—a man more concerned with "conscience" (V.ii.56-66) than vengeance. It is precisely that internal division between the Pagan and the Christian that unsuits him for action, indeed for Kingship. As you noted, in the graveyard scene it is Alexander and Caesar who are consigned to dusty mortality. What do they have in common? They were the two greatest soldiers of antiquity—men of action who would have slain Claudius in Act 1, scene 2—and they were pagan. When Hamlet goes metaphysical, as he does with Yorick, he is yearning to go Christian. So too in the "quintessence of dust" speech.

If Hamlet were a little more pagan, he would have dispatched Claudius in Act 3, scene 3 ("Now might I do it pat"). If he were a little more Christian, he would have gotten the hell out of barbarous Helsingor. As a pagan, he lives in historical time, and it is his duty to set that time right. As a Christian, he hopes to transcend historical time, and it is his duty to save his immortal soul. But in neither case can we say of Hamlet what Adorno says of modernism: "Now modern art is different from all previous art in that its mode of negation is different. Previously, styles and artistic practices were negated by new styles and practices. Today, however, modernism negates tradition itself." Hamlet not only does not negate tradition itself. He acts to uphold it.

JS: I don't see how Adorno's view has any weight when it comes to either *Ulysses* or *The Waste Land*. Neither work negates tradition. They digest it thoroughly, as Eliot claimed in his famous essay. Modernism negating Tradition? I should have thought that these two seminal works of modernism were at once thoroughly Traditional and utterly Individual. Negating and blithely forgetful texts are superficial and boring.

RB: *Ulysses* and *The Waste Land* are not *apostrophes* to the past but *apophrades*, which is to say, Joyce and Eliot have remade the tradition in their own image. When Adorno, who is nothing if not dialectical, speaks of "negating" the past, he does not mean that we should forget it, but sublate it in the Hegelian sense. That sublation necessarily involves some selective—or if you prefer—active forgetting.

And it is to "active forgetting" that I'd like to return—not as a literary phenomenon but as a way of Being-in-the-world. You began by observing that the person who makes the shopping list is not the same person who later reads it. Presumably in the case of the shopper whatever forgetting occurs is more accidental than active. But your notion that such forgetting is at once "disturbing" and "liberating" gets us to Nietzsche. So please explain. What in your view is desirable about active forgetting, and how do we weigh the "uses" against the "abuses" in an age that suffers from historical amnesia, and where the average attention span is the length of a tweet.

JS: If that's what Adorno's dialectic amounts to, it sounds awfully close to Eliot's theory and closer still to Bloom's "revisionary ratios." I'm not sure I could slide a piece of printer-paper between them.

As for my pet-category of "active forgetting," I would in fact prefer to think of it as a life-force, a well-spring of creativity, a locus of meaning and a source of intoxication. It allows one to be drunken continually on the stars, on virtue, on the single-malt of metaphor—what you will. It is a necessary paradox in referring to a deliberative forgetting (that's not to say *conscious*, necessarily). In *Thus Spake Zarathustra*, Nietzsche refers to the highest of the three spirits as the "child spirit"—a spirit of effortless, innocent forgetting, a self-perpetuating wheel, an everlasting Yea, an orgasmic Yes if one wishes to put the bloom back into Molly. Active forgetting is not the opposite of memory: it is the opposite of Freud's dreary *parapraxis*—memory as a slip of the tongue or pen, a pathology of everyday life. But surely the end of therapy is a flowering forgetfulness, a way of dismissing one's childhood horrors and other repressions, swatting them away like flies, as the old gods once killed us for sport.

Active forgetting bears no relation to the historical amnesia you rue and decry. That slavish, reflexive and above all insipid form of forgetting augurs no innocence, inseminates no joyful wisdom, creates no new value. Molly's ecstatic Yes, Joyce's blooming prose style, and Eliot's breeding lilacs out of the dead land—those are the achievement of a truly active forgetting.

RB: Adorno's theory of aesthetics—especially his engagement with Kant—is, I think, different from Eliot's and Bloom's, but those differences need not detain us here. Nietzsche penned *On the Uses and Disadvantages of History for Life*—the Second of the *Untimely Meditations*—at a time when history reigned supreme in the German academy and Leopold von Ranke was its presiding diety. Ranke's famous formulation—that history should be guided by the principle of *wie es eigentlich gewesen* ["how it actually happened"] led to an obsession with antiquarianism and archivalism. It was against this dusty and musty historical sensibility—one that prized positivism above everything and refused to see the past in dialectical relation to the present—that Nietzsche raised his voice in protest. But one suspects that if our most antithetical of philosophers were alive today he might well argue the opposite. In an epoch that remembers nothing of the past and sees the future as an empty horizon, is active forgetting of any use? Have we become so contemporary, that we have destroyed both Tradition and the Individual Talent? And, just to add a little back-spin to these questions, how does our old friend Plato—who at least metaphorically described all of knowledge as *remembering*—figure into all of this?

JS: I see your point and think we covered some of this ground in our dialogue on the Benighted States. Emerson—whom Nietzsche admired—said "Americans are blessed with amnesia," but he was thinking in a creative, not a moo-cow, register about how a certain kind of amnesia (forgetting Europe) was essential if America was to keep re-inventing itself. If our contemporaries are too lazy or stupid to remember anything about history, then—as Santayana observed—they will indeed be condemned to repeat the past whilst being utterly clueless that they are doing so.

As for Plato, his *mythos* of memory was just that: a beguiling story about how we forget everything at birth and must be reminded of the truth, philosophical dialectic being a good electric prod to make us recall our Prenatal Mingling with the Forms. It is in the Myth of Er at the end of *Republic* that Lethe begins its stream of unconsciousness, allowing the dead to forget their former lives and be reincarnated. But this is the stuff of *mythos*, not *logos*.

I want to know how you have sorted out the memory/forgetting dialectic as an existential dynamic. Kierkegaard thought *Don Giovanni* was the best opera ever written because it presents such a stirring example of creative forgetfulness, a bubbly aria of *erōs-thanatos* where forgetting spills over the Don—and us—and reminds us that memory is the devil that drags us to hell.

RB: Er is the Jesus/Finnegan of Greece: the resurrected dead man, the mortal who communes with the immortals, not to mention the eternal forms. As for memory and forgetting, Plato is—seen from one perspective—the opposite not of Nietzsche but of John Locke: we begin with a *tabula plena* rather than a *tabula rasa*. Still, I remain curious about the *mythos* of *anamnē sis* or knowledge-as-memory. In the *Meno*, Socrates shows how a lowly slave can, with a little dialectical prompting, intuitively

grasp something as recondite as geometry. I wonder if *anamnē sis* is a metaphor for a certain kind of introspection, one that leads to a knowledge so real and true that it feels intuitive—i.e., feels as though it is something we have always known. On this reading, Platonic remembering is not knowledge per se, but the innate capacity that reasoning beings have for achieving such knowledge.

In another vein, you suggest that Mozart's Don Giovanni presents a stirring example of creative forgetfulness. If so, then why does he insist that Leporello meticulously record each and every one of his conquests (*mille e tres*)? The Don does not engage in the dialectical remembering-and-forgetting that we discussed in Nietzsche, Eliot, Joyce, Adorno and Bloom, an intricately choreographed dance between past and present. Rather, he simply empties his mind—and his gonads—with every new woman, and then has his servant add a notch to his bed-post. The Don is a melancholy figure, a precursor of our contemporary hook-up culture, which is more about men bragging to men than about men loving women. He is a perfect example of the shopper who forgets what is on his list, because the list is utterly forgettable. Donna Anna, Donna Julia and Zerlina might as well be cans of soup or tubes of toothpaste. He has always already forgotten them.

JS: It is not the man that interests me. It's the music. I agree with you about the silly man and his shopping list, memorialized in Leporello's catalogue aria. Kierkegaard was wild not about the figure of Don Giovanni, but about the power and vitality of Mozart's operatic treatment of that figure. To speak of DG as a cautionary tale about the dangers of womanizing is feckless moralizing. I won't have it!

But let's return to Plato. I like what you say about the memory-myth being a metaphor for both introspection and intuition. I don't think Plato—hardly a literalist—would defend the idea that our first souls mingled with the *eidoi* and then forgot them at birth. Surely that's a good story about what it feels like to hit on a thought or have an intuition—that wildly exciting blend of Aha and Eureka and *déjà vu*. I think Plato lovingly depicts Socrates in mid-insight, self-arrested for hours on some *stoa* or other, to

give us the first model of the Intellectual, the one who wrestles with himself between his ears: a mental Milo. That kind of mental *agon* spills into the *agora*, and the rest is the history of Western philosophy.

RB: I have no interest in moralizing over the Don—I wish him well as he fucks his way through another thousand *señoritas*—but I also have no interest in romanticizing him. His forgetting is a matter not of creativity but indifference, even boredom. As for the music, yes, that is a different matter. Never before or since has there been such a brilliant orchestration of aural remembering and forgetting, a summation of all previous music transformed into something startlingly new and unique. But Mozart is no modern. So far from annulling tradition, he becomes its ultimate expression. It is because Mozart perfected a certain musical idiom that Beethoven and Wagner needed to reinvent it, becoming in the process the first musical moderns.

As for Plato, you state the matter beautifully. Lost in the architecture of his own thought, his is a wandering that is also a home-coming, a *peripatētikos* in which every logical twist and turn is at once a discovery and a recovery. He is the intellectual's Homer—his *Iliad* the *agon* of dialectic, his *Odyssey* the *nostos* of *anamnēsis*.

We seem to agree that Plato uses memory to construct Western metaphysics and Nietzsche uses forgetting to deconstruct it. And we've talked about how the moderns and the philosophers handle memory/forgetting. But what about the Romantics? Wordsworth seems to stand at one end of this opposition, Byron at the other. Are they the Plato and Nietzsche of nineteenth-century English poetry?

JS: In fact, Nietzsche deeply admired Byron and saw him—along with Napoleon and Goethe—as artistic versions of the *Übermensch*. I think Byron's early *Sturm und Drang* appealed to Nietzsche no less than Byron's frisky *ottava rima*, his book of laughter and forgetting called *Don Juan*. Byron claimed that memory gave him no pleasure, and it's no accident that his ironic masterpiece is a long, highly digressive (forgetful) narra-

tive poem about Europe's greatest playboy. The brio and élan of Mozart's opera suffuse the comic ingenuity and effervescence of *Don Juan*. The eponymous hero of our poem is, of course, a thousand times less interesting and exciting than the ingenious narrator (Byron), who is—as the poet said—"quietly facetious about everything." Memory-haunted (and anointed) Wordsworth hated every molecule of the mock-epic but kept his own book of *gravitas* and memory (*The Prelude*) under lock and key until he died in 1850. Yes, Byron and Wordsworth are the Evil Twins of British Romanticism. The river of memory runs through all of Wordsworth's best poems, but Byron drinks his epic from Lethe:

> And if I laugh at any mortal thing,
> 'Tis that I may not weep; and if I weep
> 'Tis that our nature cannot always bring
> Itself to apathy, for we must steep
> Our hearts first in the depths of Lethe's spring
> Ere what we least wish to behold will sleep.
> Thetis baptized her mortal son in Styx;
> A mortal mother would on Lethe fix. (*Don Juan* IV, 4)

The best way to put to sleep our mortal woes is to practice forgetfulness, a fully active, vital and creative forgetting that liberates us from too much memory, too much antiquarianism, too much slavish adherence to rules, regulations and other nightmares that keep us from dreaming up news that stays news. Only a heart well-steeped in Lethe will spring to Life.

RB: You have eloquently pleaded Byron's case for forgetting. But what's the other side of the dialectic—of Wordsworthian memory? The author of "Tintern Abbey" is arguably the first great poet of temporal relativity, the precursor to Proust, Mann, Joyce and Woolf. His "spots of time" anticipate Joyce's epiphany, and his preference for *kairos* over *chronos* looks forward to Beckett. Where do you locate Wordsworth in relation to Plato? Are Wordsworth's "clouds of glory" simply another version of Plato's *anamnēsis*?

JS: The verse paragraph you cite comes from the "Intimations Ode":

Our birth is but a sleep and a forgetting:
The Soul that rises with us, our life's Star,
Hath had elsewhere its setting,
And cometh from afar:
Not in entire forgetfulness,
And not in utter nakedness,
But trailing clouds of glory do we come
From God, who is our home:
Heaven lies about us in our infancy!
Shades of the prison-house begin to close
Upon the growing Boy,
But He beholds the light, and whence it flows,
He sees it in his joy;
The Youth, who daily farther from the east
Must travel, still his Nature's Priest,
And by the vision splendid
Is on his way attended;
At length the Man perceives it die away,
And fade into the light of common day.

It does sound rather Platonic but it also sounds Heideggerian. We gradually lose the ability to see the "world apparelled in celestial light." That forgetfulness is not really what Nietzsche meant by *Vergesslichkeit*. It is its pedestrian cousin. It is "common" forgetting. Perhaps a typology of memory-and- forgetting should be wagered. For certainly Kierkegaard was right to see every act of memory as a creative forgetting insofar as memory is selective, a sculptor releasing from the marble of memory a specific form. I think Wordsworth hoped that "the child is the father of the man" and located in that suggestive paradox the only way that "clouds of glory" will trail us into deadening adulthood. There is something at once childish and childlike about that hope. Byronic hope is based on *amor fati*, a Greek and Nietzschean love of fate that keeps regenerating us precisely by keeping us awash in Lethe. Ultimately, these ambitions are different ways of sculpting *chronos* into *kairos*. Byron so feared *chronos* devouring him that he lived ten lifetimes in his thirty-six years. Wordsworth hobbled to eighty and never stopped tinkering with his one-man epic about the growth of his own mind.

RB: Perhaps Wordsworth's "celestial light" has more to do with Heidegger's truth-as-unforgetting (*alētheia*) than with Plato's knowledge-as-recollection (*anamnēsis*). Here the German distinction between *Vergesslichkeit* (forgetfulness) and *Vergessenheit* (oblivion) is perhaps relevant. The former indicates a forgetting that is partial and selective, while the latter refers to a comprehensive failure of memory, one in which the individual doesn't simply forget but loses virtually all awareness or consciousness of a thing.

Heidegger is alive to this distinction in "Anaximander's Saying," where he writes "The oblivion of Being (*Seinsvergessenheit*) is the oblivion *(Vergessenheit)* of the difference between Being and beings." What does Heidegger mean in this cryptic formulation? I think he means that when we forget the difference between "Being and beings" we forget our prelinguistic origins, our experience of the world before it was contained within those categories of language that enable us to apprehend objects, actions, relations—in short "beings."

And where does Wordsworth fit into this? He tells us that the soul comes not "in entire forgetfulness" or "utter nakedness," but "trailing clouds of glory." But how is this possible? If we do not and cannot have prelinguistic memories—if language is the necessary precondition for all mental activity—then how can we ever recover the "celestial light" of Being? Wordsworth, Nietzsche and Heidegger all propose the same answer: we remember the difference between Being and beings by remembering that man is an "artistically creating subject." Once we accept the contingency of language, once we acknowledge that our empirical codes are "made" rather than "found," then we can understand the essential connection between *aesthetics* and *aisthanesthai*, between our capacity to perceive beauty and the processes of sensuous perception itself. Here is how Nietzsche puts the matter in "On Truth and Lies in a Nonmoral Sense":

> Only by forgetting [*Vergessen*] this primitive world of metaphor can one live with any repose, security, and consistency: only by means of the petrification and coagulation of a mass of images which originally streamed from the primal faculty of human imagination like a fiery liquid, only in the invincible faith that *this* sun,

> *this* window, *this* table is a truth in itself, in short only by forgetting that he is himself an *artistically creating* subject, does man live with any repose, security and consistency.

Notice that here Nietzsche recommends neither *Vergessenheit* nor *Vergesslichkeit* but *Erinnerung* (memory). To break out of the routine of settled usage, to live as an artistically creating subject rather than in security and repose is to *remember* the contingency of language. Nietzsche is, for once, in the same camp as Heidegger and Wordsworth. But I'm left wondering what to do with Plato. Certainly Heidegger is riffing on him when he transforms "recollection" into "unforgetting"?

JS: I scent theoretical fantasy the way Don Giovanni scents women. How could we possibly know anything about a "primitive world of metaphor"? Certainly, that is a conjecture based on what seems to have followed from it. How can we intuit anything about "the primal faculty of human imagination" except by examining what appear to be its traces, its trailing clouds? Maybe these early intuitions are what Nietzsche called "early Greek thinking" (he has a book with that title). Philosophy is clearly something that happens after the fall into secure categories. But how can we presume to know anything about the "artistically creating subject" that lived before the dawn of language?

RB: For Nietzsche and Heidegger the "traces" of primal imagination are present everywhere, recoverable like so many archeological deposits in verbal etymologies. As the linguistic paleontologist applies hammer to word, the sedimentation of usage falls away and the metaphor within stands revealed, a compact fossil of meaning. You say that you scent "theoretical fantasy" the way Don Giovanni scents a woman. Consider your metaphors, which mix the olfactory with the visual. *Fantasy* derives from *phantasia* (appearance, mental image, representation) and *phantazein* (to make visible or present to the eye or mind); *theory* comes from *theōrein* (to look at, behold, perceive, consider, contemplate), but is also related to *theōros* (spectator) and *thea* (an act of seeing—from which we get "theatre"). When Heidegger raises the question of the difference between Being and beings he is fundamentally asking how we render intelligible what is sensible; how we conceptualize (*theōrein*) our perceptions (*phantasia* is *Vorstellung*) of the world; how we "see" our own way of "seeing."

According to Nietzsche we accomplish this by unpacking the "metaphors, metonymies and anthropomorphisms" that define our world. That is why Heidegger describes language as the "House of Being," and why he believes that the poet (*Dichter*) is a species of philosopher (*Denker*). That is also why the poem the world calls "Tintern Abbey," Wordsworth called "Lines." For it is through "lines" of poetry—through language—that we know the world "Of eye, and ear—both what they half create / And what perceive."

Which returns us to the question of Plato and Heidegger. Knowledge-as-recollection (*anamnēsis*) imagines reality as intelligibility, a situation in which the poet is superfluous. Truth-as-unforgetting imagines reality as sensibility, a situation in which the poet is supreme. Under the circumstances, I think we can agree that Wordsworth's "remembering" is more Heideggerian than Platonic, yes?

JS: I think the "Intimations Ode" traces and trails its sensuous hints of immortality taken from the childhood of the imagination, and the "celestial light" that once "appareled" the world is precisely the world in which we do not forget to ask the question of Being. So I would agree that there is something Heideggerian about Wordsworthian remembering-and-forgetting. But I have to say I prefer the poet's lyric evocations to the philosopher's more abstruse musings and jargon. But so did Heidegger. Poetry jars Being into place, the better to see it. Philosophy theorizes from a necessary distance, a canny spectator but not even close to the gazelle, leaping, sipping the liquid horizon.

Regarding that horizon of intuition, let me wonder/wander a little as we perhaps reach to the end. A riverruns through all our intuitions, from that metaphorical *jouissance* of early Greek thinking (Thales babbled that all is Water!) to the spontaneous overflows of Wordsworth, to the novelistic rejoicing that allows us to spring into streams of consciousness, nourishing the blooms of an everlasting Yea. Mnemosyne and Lethe form a confluence in these evocations and intuitions as beautifully mysterious, as piquant and profound, as the shopping list I just fished out, written by someone else called "James" an age ago.

RB: Heidegger wrote abstracted poetry and Wordsworth wrote distracted philosophy. Must we choose between their anecdotal jarrings, between the "dominion" they achieved over the "slovenly wilderness," whether in Todtnauberg or Grasmere?

As for Mnemosyne and Lethe, you launch them breast-by-breast into the River of Recollection, a couple of sleek mermaids in a synchronized swimming competition, each sounding bells on the buoys of culture as they proceed around their watery course. But I prefer to envision our dynamic duo as a couple of superannuated bathing beauties from yesteryear, drowsily sunning themselves on a litter-strewn beach, one nostalgically clutching a photo album in her liver-spotted hands, the other droolingly lost in the age-addled limbo of incipient Alzheimer's. Do they achieve "confluences" of "evocation and intuition," or does each remain enclosed in her solitary world of self-regard?

You conclude (shades of Carlyle and Molly Bloom) with the everlasting Yea. Stranded as I am in the American Heartland I would rather end—as I suspect I shall—with the everlasting Moo. Here is Nietzsche's description of the confrontation between the history-haunted man who remembers and the care-free cow who forgets: "A human being may well ask the animal: 'Why do you not speak to me of your happiness but only stand and gaze at me.' The animal would like to answer, and say: 'The reason is I always forget what I was going to say'—but then he forgot this answer too, and stayed silent."

JS: To amend Wittgenstein, if a moo-cow could speak, we would not be able to understand it. Its form of life—and its form of forgetfulness—are unspeakable.

Socrates Among the Cicadas: The Art of the Platonic Dialogue

JS: At Monticello in 1814, while designing the University of Virginia—that neo-classical masterpiece he called "an academical village"—Thomas Jefferson wrote to John Adams:

> I am just returned from one of my long absences, having been at my other home for five weeks past. Having more leisure there than here for reading, I amused myself with reading seriously Plato's Republic. I am wrong however in calling it amusement, for it was the heaviest task-work I ever went through. I had occasionally before taken up some of his other works, but scarcely ever had patience to go through a whole dialogue. While wading thro' the whimsies, the puerilities, and unintelligible jargon of this work, I laid it down often to ask myself how it could have been that the world should have so long consented to give reputation to such nonsense as this?

Jefferson wisely surmises that Plato became "canonized" by the early Church fathers who saw in his mysticism the first tremblings of Christianity. Thus Platonism becomes grafted onto the simple teachings of Jesus to give them a classical pedigree.

But is Jefferson generally right about Plato's "unintelligible jargon"? Jefferson was no doubt reading *Republic* in Greek, so his views are not tainted by the treacle of translation. Jefferson claims—he is not alone in the charge—that Plato was a Sophist, despite how much Plato despised the Sophists. Far from practicing a subtle, supple dialectic, Plato's Socrates will go to any lengths to make his weaker argument appear the stronger—that is, to put his dialogic opponent in more and more untenable positions, no matter how absurd his own position became in the process.

How to cite this book chapter:
Begam, R. and Soderholm, J. 2015. Socrates Among the Cicadas: The Art of the Platonic Dialogue. In: Begam, R. and Soderholm, J. *Platonic Occasions: Dialogues on Literature, Art and Culture*. Pp. 159–176. Stockholm: Stockholm University Press. DOI: http://dx.doi.org/10.16993/sup.baa.j.

Was Plato "of the Sophist's party without knowing it"? And how much do our own dialogues represent a series of necessary footnotes to Plato? Or have we, in the preceding dialogues, engaged in a properly dialectical way of thinking? Does it finally take *two* minds to tango philosophically?

RB: There are two Platos: the didactic Plato of *Republic, Crito, Phaedo* and *Timaeus* and the ludic Plato of *Symposium, Phaedrus, Theaetetus* and *Sophist*. Which is the "true" Plato and which the "false"? Happily we need not choose. As Plato himself observes in *Sophist,* "when we say *that which is not*, we don't say something contrary [*enantion*] to *that which is*, but only something different [*alla*] from it" (257 b). Just as there is no single Shakespeare, there is no single Plato.

That Jefferson, Founder of the American Republic, regarded Plato's *Republic* as "whimsical," "puerile" and "unintelligible" is no surprise. *The Declaration of Independence* and the *Constitution of the United States* stand as far from *The Republic*—or *Politeia* ["civil polity," "form of government"] to give Plato's work its proper name—as Obama's Washington does from Pericles' Athens. Of course, the most influential negative account of *Politeia* came from Karl Popper, who argued that Plato's work provided a blueprint for twentieth-century totalitarianism. Eric Voeglin, Leo Strauss and Allan Bloom all persuasively answered, each in his own way, Popper's crude and reductive reading.

I myself like to imagine *Politeia* as a kind of utopic-dystopic novel, Plato's version of Book IV of *Gulliver's Travels*. Plato could never forgive Athenian democracy for having murdered his teacher and arguably the greatest man of the age. Having sweepingly condemned all forms of Greek government—timocracy, oligarchy, democracy and tyranny—he proposes an alternative that abolishes family, censors poetry and art, places men and women on an equal footing (a scandalous thought in Plato's time) and strikes at both aristocracy (men of "gold" may rise beyond their appointed rank, 415 a-b) and private property. In other words, he writes a book designed to offend *everyone*. What better way for Plato to vent his spleen against the city that killed Socrates?

JS: Re-reading *Theaetetus* this morning I found myself writing (mentally) in the margins: "surpassingly clever; insufficiently dialectical." In terms both congenial and hostile to Socrates, I might accuse Plato/Socrates of being a disingenuous midwife, posing as someone who helps others to give birth to the truth, when in fact he is delivering *himself* of an entire nursery of Ideas. But in the other works you mention, Plato is more of a literary man and more or less convincingly dialectical. That raises the question of how seriously we can take his banishing of poets when Plato himself so often avails himself of figurative language, similes and allegories. Indeed, arguably his most famous glimpse of the form of the Good is presented in/as the allegory of the cave. We recall that *allēgoria* is a "saying otherwise" or a "speaking differently" (this also accounts, in Greek, for Plato's using the *alias* of Socrates in the *agora*). Like Emily Dickinson, Plato is telling the truth, if not the Truth, but telling it slant. He is not "saying the thing which is not" but rather suggestively evoking *logos* in and through *mythos*—the dialectic as "hypotheses, underpinnings, footings, springboards" (*Politeia* VI, 511b-c).

It is difficult to imagine that Jefferson dismissed these inspired moments of *mythos* as "whimsies." But Jefferson could have pointed to dozens and dozens of passages where Plato seems about as dialectically nimble as Polonius. Before turning to *Politeia* and its mixture of logic-chopping banality—not to mention, winged allegories and elastic springboards—let me detain you for a moment with a passage from *Theaetetus*.

> THEAETETUS: Really, I am not sure, Socrates. I cannot even make out about you, whether you are stating this as something you believe or merely putting me to the test.
> SOCRATES: You forget, my friend, that I know nothing of such matters and cannot claim to be producing any offspring of my own. I am only trying to deliver yours, and to that end uttering charms over you and tempting your appetite with a variety of delicacies from the table of wisdom, until by my aid your own belief shall be brought to light. Once that is done, I shall see whether it proves to have some life in it or not. Meanwhile, have courage and patience and answer my questions bravely in accordance with your convictions.
> THEAETETUS: Go on with your questioning. (157 c-d)

But is Plato—alias Socrates—really being the dialectical, midwifely equivalent of an "honest broker" here? He asks ridiculously leading, tempting and taunting questions in order to maneuver his interlocutors into more and more untenable positions. Can this nettling and hectoring really be passed off as midwifery? Or is the pose of the midwife one of the aliases by which the truth speaks *otherwise*, or *differently*? Is that variable, ambiguous position of the Socratic inquisitor midway between *logos* and *mythos*, the forward slash [/] eliding "either" and "or" and suggesting that Theaetetus (as well as the reader) must court the possibility that "what one believes" and "putting others to the test" are the yin and yang of Platonic dialectic? In other words, "Praise *alla* ..."

RB: The maieutic conceit frames *Theaetetus*. Socrates' interlocutor begins by confessing his inability to answer the question "What is knowledge [*epistēmē*]?" but Socrates reassures him, suggesting that he is "big with idea":

> SOCRATES: This isn't lack of fertility, Theaetetus. You're pregnant, and these are your labor-pains.
> THEAETETUS: I don't know about that, Socrates. I'm just telling you my experiences.
> SOCRATES: Don't be so serious! Haven't you heard that my mother Phainarete was a good, sturdy midwife [*maias*]?
> THEAETEUS: Yes, somebody did tell me once.
> SOCRATES: And have you heard that I practice the same profession? (148e-149a)

By the end of the dialogue, Socrates, having demonstrated the insufficiency of all theories of knowledge, returns to the metaphor of midwifery:

> SOCRATES: Well, are we still pregnant? Is anything relevant to knowledge still causing us pain, my friend, or have we given birth to everything?
> THEAETETUS: *I* most certainly have: thanks to you. I've put into words more than I had in me.
> SOCRATES: And does our midwifery declare that everything we produced was still-born and that there was nothing worth keeping?

> THEAETETUS: Absolutely.
> SOCRATES: Well, Theaetetus, if you set out at a later date to conceive more ideas, and you succeed, the ideas with which you'll be pregnant will be better because of this inquiry of ours; and even if you don't get pregnant, you'll be easier to get on with, because you won't make a nuisance of yourself by thinking that you know what you don't know. This *sōphrosunē* [soundness of mind, moderation, discretion] is all my skill is capable of giving, nothing more. (210b-c)

One of Plato's great themes is that Socrates' ultimate wisdom consists in knowing only that he does not know, and at 155d Socrates commends Theaetetus' own admission of ignorance as the basis for philosophy itself: "It looks as though Theodorus' sketch of your character was accurate, my friend. I mean, this feeling—a sense of wonder [*thauma*]—is perfectly proper to a philosopher: philosophy has no other foundation, in fact."

So is Socrates genuinely maieutic or does he simply give birth to his own ideas? By reminding us that Socrates follows his mother's profession, Plato may be slyly suggesting that his teacher's famous method is a form of intellectual autogenesis—that the offspring of Socrates' midwifery is none other than Socrates himself. But does it matter? Socrates is examining himself as much as his interlocutor. Indeed, in the *Sophist*, he defines the very object of philosophy—thinking [*dianoia*]—as "the soul's conversation with itself" (264a). And as I needn't tell you, the Greek word for conversation is *dialogia*.

All of which is to say, I find *Theaetetus* both surpassingly clever and surpassingly dialectical. As for your last question—is maieutics a method or a masquerade, a form of logic or of myth—I say Yes and Yes.

JS: Molly Bloom meets the Interior Paramour of Wallace Stevens. That coupling suggests that it takes only *one* to tango dialogically and dialectically. If so, then our own dialogues must be second-order productions, relying as they do on *two* minds wondering into discourse and debate. This discussion does make "one" wonder what we two are up to in our collection of dialogues. Let me say that I find the wisdom of Socratic ignorance so divertingly disingenuous that it must be, well, literary. Is this what you imply by your double affirmation "Yes and Yes"?

RB: Dialectic and dialogic begin in doubt, in being of two minds as the German *Zweifel* and the Italian *dubitare* suggest. Of course, one person can be of two minds, just as two people can be of one mind. For genuine dialogue to occur, what's important is not the number of participants but the nature of the activity.

The problem with the Sophist is that he knows in advance where he is going. There is no doubt, no wondering, no wandering. He hums along the highway of argument, disregarding the twists and turns demanded by logical progression and internal coherence. Ignoring the complex interplay of identity and difference—what Plato calls the "weaving together of forms" [*eidōn sumplokē*]—the Sophist separates what should be connected and connects what should be separate. In one of the truly astonishing moments in the dialogues, Socrates describes such crude logic-chopping as "the sign of a completely unmusical [*amouson*] and unphilosophical [*aphilosophon*] person" (*Sophist*, 259e). I say "astonishing" because *amouson* does not signify "unmusical" (as Nicholas White translates it) so much as "inaesthetic" or "indifferent to the Muses," which means that, here at least, Socrates gives equal weight to the claims of art and philosophy.

Then again, perhaps this moment is not so astonishing. As we have remarked, in the Platonic canon there are at least two Socrates, one of whom lingers with Phaedrus among the cicadas, those friends of the Muses who preferred art to life itself:

> The story is that these creatures were once human beings, belonging to a time before the Muses were born, and that with the birth of the Muses and the appearance of song some of the people of the time were so unhinged by the pleasure that in their singing they neglected to eat and drink and failed to notice that they had died. From them the race of the cicadas later sprang. (*Phaedrus*, 259 b-c)

JS: I am of one, two—no—many minds about your last observations. It is clear to me that our longish replies to each other in our dialogues are intellectual wanderings, divagations and investigations more or less animated (taking wing) from each other's thoughts and remarks. We are the heirs of Plato inasmuch as we hold forth like Socrates, drawing some dialectical electricity from each other but also giving birth to our own ideas. Plato did at least require the example, if not the spectacle, of Socrates pestering the hell out of Athenians in the marketplace, giving his fellow citizens a profound case of agoraphobia. Unlike the more eristic dialogues—where Socrates badgers his opponents into blandly reflexive agreement with all his views—we never reduce each other to a "yes man," despite your recent "Yes and Yes," which of course was the consummation of your Socratic peroration.

Speaking of doubt as a method of inquiry (including *dubito ergo cogito ergo sum*), I'd like to return to the passage you quoted earlier from *Theaetetus* when Socrates encourages young Theaetetus (I use the Cornford translation) "to find a single formula that applies to the many kinds of knowledge" (148d). Theaetetus explains that he has tried to do this but cannot find any satisfactory solution. "And yet," says Theaetetus, "I cannot get the question out of my mind," to which Socrates replies, "My dear Theaetetus, that is because your mind is not empty or barren. You are suffering the pains of travail" (148e). The importance of Socrates in the *polis*, and the larger point of Plato in *Politeia*, rests on how far one gets others to the point where they are fruitfully doubtful, rife with fecundating self-division and, therefore, incapable of sophistry. Hamlet epitomizes that state of mind with the most famous disjunction on the planet—"To be or not to be "—and later in the play when he says, "In my heart there was a kind of fighting that would not let me sleep." That *agōn*, that strife, is what makes Hamlet the most beautifully doubtful creature ever penned by man or god. Endlessly bemusing himself, Hamlet is the most philosophical of princes.

Indeed, Hamlet is one of those who would rather listen to the husky music of the cicadas than do something so politically-pointed as skewer Claudius. "To be or not to be"—that is the question he cannot get out of his head and his own way of weaving together forms results in his seeing man as "this quintessence of dust." Hamlet finally comes to prefer the music of his own mind (his shaped sphere, his distracted globe) to life in rotten Denmark. He is of one, two—many minds about *everything*. Is Hamlet the quintessence of Socrates?

RB: The peregrinating Prince engages in the "soul's conversation with itself," reading in the book of the self "words, words, words." To doubt is to be of more than one mind. It is to be many-minded, myriad-minded, possessed of a "negative capability" that enables the singular to become the plural. Hamlet, bounded in a nutshell, encompasses infinite space, discovering more in heaven and earth than is dreamt of in his or anyone's philosophy. But what of Plato, who in *Parmenides* and *Sophist* argues for both the One and the Many. Is he also myriad-minded?

Before becoming a philosopher, Plato tried his hand at writing tragedies, and it is worth remembering that most of his dialogues are polylogues, closet dramas complete with characters, settings and actions. *Euthyphro, Apology*, *Crito* and *Phaedo* constitute a tetralogy, which tells the tragic story of the death of Athens' greatest citizen. Like Achilles, Socrates is given a choice between glory and ignominy, and like Achilles he chooses the noble course, a point Plato drives home in *Crito* (44b) when he compares Socrates to the hero of *The Iliad*.

But it is not only Plato's tetralogy that employs dramatic forms and themes. Most of the dialogues take as their title the name of a youth of noble origin, who emerges as Plato's dramatic hero and whose interrogation by Socrates constitutes the central "action" of the dialogue. Admittedly, these dramas are internalized, with conflicts and resolutions that are psychological and philosophical, but their structure is surprisingly Aristotelian. So it is that virtually every dialogue is built around a moment of *peripeteia* or reversal in which the hero is "turned around," forced to renounce a doctrinal system, whether it comes from Protagoras or Parmenides or Heraclitus. How does Plato characterize the "error" that leads the hero to "fall" into "false belief"? In *Theaetetus*, Socrates calls it *hamartia* (189c), the very word Aristotle later uses to describe the "flaw" or "error" of the tragic hero. It is especially revealing to see how Plato anatomizes *hamartia* in *Phaedrus*: "When judgement leads us by reason towards the best and is in control, its control over us has the name of restraint [*sōphrosunē*]; when desire drags us irrationally towards pleasures and has established rule within us, its rule is called by the name of excess [*hubris*]" (237e-238a). That *hubris* is the most common source of *hamartia* is a truism, it seems, not only of tragedy but also of the Platonic dialogue. And where does this internalized drama of the soul finally lead? For Aristotle tragedy achieves its critical mass, its moral and emotional coherence, in the moment of *anagnōrisis* or "recognition," when the hero finally gains "knowledge" [*gnosis*] of his situation and himself.

Most Platonic dialogues also reach their climax in a moment of *anagnōrisis* but with this difference: the young man achieves a specific kind of knowledge—a *sōphrosunē* or the "modesty" that comes from understanding the *limits* of knowledge. Here is the conclusion of *Theaetetus*, where Socrates reviews and rejects all the possible definitions of knowledge that he and his interlocutor have considered: "Therefore, Theaetetus, knowledge [*epistēmē*] can be neither perception, nor true belief, nor true belief with the addition of rational account" (210a-b). As Socrates explains in the *Apology* (20e), the Oracle of Delphi has declared him the wisest of men because he alone knows that he knows nothing. This is indeed the "ultimate" knowledge that Socrates imparts to his followers. Philosophy not only begins in wonder—in being of two minds—it ends in it.

JS: You make a strong (novelistic) case for Plato's being on the side of artists in the ancient quarrel between poetry and philosophy. Therefore, there must have been more than a touch of irony in his infamous banishment of poets from the utopian state. You have admirably depicted Plato wrestling with Homer and the tragedians for the hearts, souls and minds of the Athenians. He must outwit them at their own games, participating in a literary Olympiad where the unlikely hero is an ugly old man with bulging eyes and snub nose.

But does Plato's philosophy end in wonder? In many dialogues we are given plenty of hints to a higher wisdom that has gone far beyond doubt. The culmination of that wisdom is the theory of Forms and particularly the Form of the Good. What is peculiar is how Plato must resort to literary techniques to intimate that higher knowledge, that moment when doubtful *doxa* gives way to the excellence [*arête*] of *epistēmē*. We are not always left, that is, with Socratic irony, but sometimes with Platonic metaphysics, the recognition that one is flourishing in the sunlight of Reason, Truth and Goodness once one has emerged from the cave of shadows and illusions.

So I am forced to drive a wedge between Socrates, who wrote nothing, and Plato, who wrote voluminously, giving his teacher all his own views, standing behind him as the first term stands "behind" the second term in "Plato/Socrates." But would Socrates "stand behind" (support, endorse) *any* of Plato's metaphysical views? Is Socrates a persona for Plato the way Marlow is a persona for Conrad? These considerations necessarily bring to mind Derrida's perversely brilliant reading of the medieval depiction of Plato standing behind a scribal Socrates.

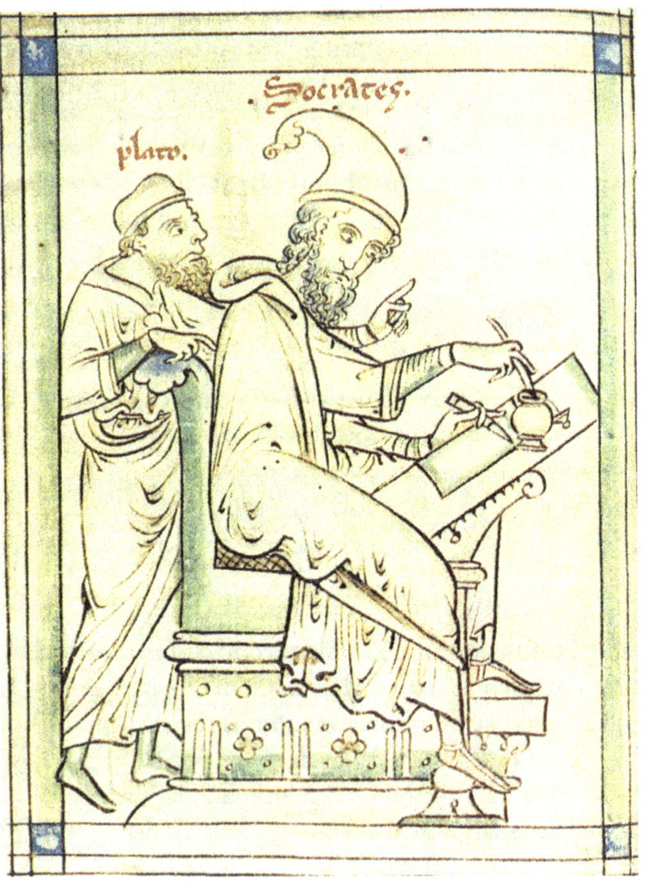

Figure 10: Frontispiece, *Prognostica Socratis Baseilei.*

A theoretically-tumescent Derrida gazes at this "post-card" and tosses off the following:

> The card immediately seemed to me, how to put it, obscene ... For the moment, myself, I tell you that I see Plato getting an erection in Socrates' back and see the insane hubris of his prick, an interminable, disproportionate erection ... slowly sliding, still warm, under Socrates' right leg ... Imagine the day, when we will be able to send sperm by post card ... [And, finally, Plato] wants to emit ... to sow the entire earth, to send the same fertile card to everyone. (*La Carte Postal*)

I will add nothing to this astonishing observation except to remark that *sōphrosunē* is in jeopardy. But whose lack of restraint is it: Plato's or Derrida's? Whose seminar is being "emitted"? Is Derrida's interpretation of the image (and the scene of writing) obscene or has he put his finger on something erotically overdetermined in the relationship between Plato and Socrates, something perhaps more subtly suggested by Socrates and Phaedrus "making love" [of wisdom] among the cicadas? So what do you make of the *visual peripeteia* of the image above and what it suggests about the literary uses—and abuses—of Socrates?

RB: My case is not for a novelistic but a theatrical Plato, one who wears masks, speaks in different voices and manipulates appearance and reality, like the wizard [*pharmakeus*] to which Socrates is compared, even as he insists that such mimetic legerdemain is a crime against the *polis*: "So if we are visited in our state by someone who has the skill to transform himself into all sorts of characters and represent all sorts of things, and he wants to show off himself and his poems to us, we shall treat him with all the reverence due to a priest and a giver of rare pleasure, but shall tell him that he and his kind have no place in our city" (*Politeia* III, 398a). Remember what Alcibiades says of Socrates: He is a Silenus (215b), whose *trompe l'oeil* exterior bears no resemblance to what lies within, a man who "spends his whole life being ironic [*eirōneuomenos*] and playing games [*paizōn*] with people" (*Symposium* 216e). Could anything be more playfully ironic than ironically banishing the player from the stage?

But, you will ask, pose and posture as Socrates does, isn't the Man behind the Mask, the God within the Silenus, the *eidos* above *eikasia*, finally a metaphysician who scolds us benighted humans out of the Cave of Illusion and into the Light of Truth? After all, Socrates's larger argument in *Theaetetus* consists in demonstrating to his young charge that the Sophists are wrong, that perception (shadowy *aisthēsis)* is neither knowledge [*epistēmē*] nor truth [*alētheia*]. Indeed, isn't Plato's condemnation of art—of the *aesthetic*—predicated on the claim that *aisthēsis* is an empty and illusory form of belief [*doxa*], the opposite of true knowledge, which is to be found only in the realm of the eternal Forms?

To which I can only say, "Yes ... but." Consider the explanation of the Forms in *Phaedrus*:

> Now the region above the heavens has never been celebrated as it deserves to be by any earthly poet, nor will it ever be. But it is like this—for one must be bold enough to say what is true, especially when speaking about truth. This region is occupied by being [*ousia*] which really is, which is without colour or shape, intangible, observable [*theatē*] by the steersman of the soul [*psuchē*] alone, by intellect [*nous*], to which the class of true knowledge [*alēthous epistēmēs*] relates. (247c-d)

Notice that Socrates does not tell us what the Platonic heaven *is*, but what it is *like*. Of particular interest is his use of the word *theatē* ["visible," "observable," "see-able"]. I said earlier that Plato's dialogues function as internalized dramas, a kind of theatre of the mind, and it is precisely this theatricality that is essential to Plato's idealism. How does one render perceptible what is colorless and shapeless? How does one look upon [*theaomai*] what cannot be looked upon [*theateos*]? One makes the *eidos* "visible" [*theatē*] by constructing a place of seeing, a *theatron* or theatre. Hence, Plato writes not merely dialogues but closet *dramas*, a marriage of literature and philosophy in which the abstract is made concrete and the concrete is made abstract. Socrates may be—to speak the language of Wittgenstein—the ladder Plato wishes to throw away. But Plato cannot reach the metaphysical high ground without him.

As for that posed card, I will be happy to comment, but I have rambled on long enough and am keen to have your own response to Derrida's "preposterous" reading.

JS: That your theatrical Socrates would be banished forthwith from Plato's rational utopia is a gymnastic irony unappreciated—and indeed undetected—by most philosophers. And by theologians for that matter. The wholly, holy and ineffable nature of Plato's Good is precisely what made it so suggestive to the early Church Fathers who wanted to see in Greek philosophy the germ or embryo of Christian metaphysics. Paul had no trouble making the Unknown God on the Areopagus into the One, True God. That was awfully clever and opportunistic of him. The idea of a "theatrical Plato" who performs all the tricks you mention would have been anathema to Aquinas and St. Augustine, not to mention Plotinus, that reverential and deeply humorless repriser of Platonic ideas. But I do think there is something reductive and dismissive about treating Plato's ideas divorced from their dramatically-signifying contexts. And you are right to remark his necessarily figural commitments as he tries to intimate the intelligible realm in and through material gleaned from the visible realm (the divided line is caught in the loop of metaphor). As Lacan says to St. Paul's "The Letter killeth but the Spirit giveth life"—"Yes, but how does Spirit live except in the Letter?"

Plato's "ladder of love" in *Phaedrus* is most efficiently—and amusingly—reconstructed (in reverse, no less) in one of my favorite moments from Byron's comic masterpiece:

> 'Tis the perception of the beautiful
> A fine extension of the faculties,
> Platonic, universal, wonderful,
> Drawn from the stars, and filter'd through the skies,
> Without which life would be extremely dull;
> In short, it is the use of our own eyes,
> With one or two small senses added, just
> To hint that flesh is form'd of fiery dust. (*Don Juan* II, 212)

"[F]iltered through the skies" of allegory and simile, Plato's *kaloi* reach down into our fiery flesh and quicken our impulses for both *erōs* and *epistēmē*. That is the genius of the dialogues and their dialectic at their best. The mental theatre you suggest is "drawn from the stars" but it is also very much staged for our sensuous enjoyment. A contradiction—or an ancient quarrel—emerges between philosophy and literature only insofar as we take seriously Plato's most astringent pronouncement against poetry and poets in *Politeia*. But this still leaves us with the meaning of that damned postcard.

RB: My reading of Derrida's reading: fantasy and self-projection. Derrida would like to do to Plato what he accuses Plato of doing to Socrates. He deliberately takes him the wrong way, turns him around, reverses him. Hence Platonic insemination—see *Phaedrus*—becomes Derridean dissemination; Platonic erection—mental and physical—becomes Derridean deconstruction. But the Jacques therapy doesn't quite come off. It leaves the Frenchman, rather than the two Greeks, looking limp: an unhappy instance of *hamartia* or "missing the mark."

As for the Church Fathers, I have no doubt that they would have shuttered the Platonic theatre, had they recognized it, just as surely as the Puritans shuttered the English theatre in 1642. Presumably they read a dialogue like *Phaedrus* selectively, turning a blind eye to those moments when the Platonic flesh catches fire: "Once [the lover] has received the emanation of beauty through his eyes, he grows warm, and through the perspiration that ensues, he irrigates the sprouting of his wing. When he is quite warm, the outer layers of the seedling unfurls ... [and] as nourishment streams upon it the stump of the wing begins to swell and grow from the root upward as a support for the entire structure of the soul" (251b). What, one wonders, would Thomas Aquinas have made of a passage like this?

Of course, if sensuous apprehension [*aisthēsis*] is continuous with spiritual knowledge, if the ladder of *erōs* leads to the heaven of *eidos*, then are we dealing with a fully aestheticized Plato, with a Socrates who not only lingers among the cicadas but also luxuriates in them? Nietzsche acknowledges the dramatic element in the dialogues, but he rejects the aesthetic reading:

> Socrates, the dialectical hero of the Platonic drama, reminds us of the kindred nature of the Euripedean hero who must defend his actions with arguments and counterarguments and in the process often risks the loss of our tragic pity; for who could mistake the *optimistic* element in the nature of dialectic, which celebrates a triumph with every conclusion and can breathe only in cool clarity and consciousness—the optimistic element which, having once penetrated tragedy must gradually overgrow its Dionysian regions and impel it necessarily to self-destruction—to the death-leap into bourgeois drama ... Optimistic dialectic drives *music* out of tragedy with the scourge of syllogisms; that is, it destroys the essence of tragedy. (*Birth of Tragedy*, section 14)

What are the limits to treating Plato as a Friend of the Muses as well as of the Forms? Does dialectic finally undermine drama by rationalizing and systematizing it? It is perhaps worth pointing out that when Socrates speaks of the cicadas "conversing" among themselves, the verb he uses is *dialegesthai* (259a): "to engage in dialectic."

JS: Like Derrida's projection-fantasy in *La Carte Postale*, Nietzsche's reading of Socrates in "The Problem of Socrates" is also laced with the author's own profound anxieties and misgivings about his "position" as a philosopher in a cultural (and academic) environment deeply suspicious of his ideas. "The Problem of Socrates" begins to look like a double-portrait: of Socrates (the "Jew against Greek civilization") and of Nietzsche (the mad professor against the decay of European civilization). Both philosophers are speaking unpleasant truths, presenting untimely meditations and remarking the twilight of various idols, in Nietzsche's case the death of God Himself. Nietzsche's following remarks are wonderfully intriguing in this regard:

> Is the irony of Socrates an expression of revolt? Of plebeian *ressentiment?* Does he, as one oppressed, enjoy his own ferocity in the knife thrusts of his argument? Does he avenge himself on the noble audience he fascinates? As a dialectician, he holds a merciless tool in his hand; he can become a tyrant by means of it; he compromises those he conquers. The dialectician leaves it to his opponent

> to prove that he is not an idiot: he enrages and neutralizes his opponent at the same time. The dialectician renders the intellect of his opponent powerless. Indeed, in Socrates, is dialectic only a form of revenge?
>
> I have explained how it was that Socrates could repel: it is therefore all the more necessary to explain how he could fascinate. That he discovered a new kind of contest, that he became its first fencing master for the noble circles of Athens, is one point. He fascinated by appealing to the competitive impulse of the Greeks—he introduced a variation into the wrestling match between young men and youths. Socrates was a great erotic. (*Twilight of the Idols*, 7-8)

The role of Socrates as erotic dialectician is what makes *Phaedrus* such compelling reading. I think you're right to observe that Nietzsche ignores—or represses—the "aesthetic Socrates" but he does acknowledge the erotic dimension of the ugly, old Greek, his capacity to fire up Athenian youths by demonstrating to them the distinctive pleasures in the *agōn*[y] of dialectical repartee, particularly when those intellectual debates occur in olive groves, the whirring music of the cicadas inspiring the husky melodies of Socrates and his beautiful pupil in conversation. Like cicadas, they forget to eat and drink, so ravishing is the sound of their own minds in concert. Both early theologians and, for that matter, Nietzsche, are deaf to that sensuously-rational music. The "two Platos" you mentioned earlier in this dialogue are reduced to one, who is either a forerunner of Christian asceticism or Nietzsche's resentful logician who likes to stab people with arguments. The aesthetical, "literary" Plato we have been discussing understood that *erōs*, *eidos* and *epistēmē* are dialectical kissing cousins, as hard to separate as dancer and dance.

RB: I take Nietzsche's reading of Socrates more seriously than I do Derrida's comments on the post card. Certainly there is a case to be made for the proposition that in Euripedean tragedy—ironic, dialectical, polemical—Socrates has replaced Dionysos and Apollo as the reigning deity of the Attic stage. I wouldn't say that Nietzsche represses the "aesthetic" Socrates, but that he regards this Socrates as overly and aridly Apollinian: "Now we should be able to come closer to the character of *aesthetic Socratism*, whose supreme law reads roughly as follows, 'To be beautiful everything must be intelligible,' as counterpart to the Socratic dictum, 'Knowledge is virtue'" (*Birth of Tragedy*, section 12).

But here I think Nietzsche errs, for, as we have discussed, the Socratic dictum is not "Knowledge is virtue" but "Knowledge of one's ignorance is virtue," the *sōphrosunē* that enables dialectic wondering and wandering. That Nietzsche is also, as you point out, anxiously positioning himself in relation to his own time and place further complicates his brilliant but tendentious insights into Plato. Nietzsche's self-projection becomes unmistakable in *Birth of Tragedy* when he addresses the question of whether an "artistic Socrates" is possible: "For with respect to art that despotic logician occasionally had the feeling of a gap, a void, half a reproach, possibly a neglected duty. As he tells his friends in prison, there often came to him one and the same dream apparition, which always said the same thing to him: 'Socrates, practice music'" (section 14). In the Greek, "practice music" is *mousikēn poiei*, which might better be translated as "Dedicate yourself to the Muses!" or more simply "Create art!" (*Phaedo*, 60e). Later Nietzsche returns to this moment in *Crito*, speculating on the prospects for a contemporary "artistic Socrates," who would philosophize not with a hammer but a tuning fork: "Here we knock, deeply moved, at the gates of present and future: will this 'turning' lead to ever-new configurations of genius and especially of the *Socrates who practices music?*" (section 15). The "turning" or *peripeteia* that Nietzsche contemplates—casting himself in the role of an artistic Socrates—would have the happy effect of restoring a proper balance to the Apollinian and the Dionysian, to thought and feeling, philosophy and art.

One wonders what Jefferson, if he had summoned the "patience" to "go through a whole dialogue," would have made of such a Socrates, one who dedicates himself to the Muses, one who creates art.

JS: It is more and more apparent to me that Jefferson was not on the alert for those literary dimensions of Plato's thought you have so ably adumbrated and celebrated in the last few pages.

Perhaps *Symposium* or *Phaedrus* would have stimulated his interest a bit more. *Politeia* can be a dreadful bore at times, particularly in the early books where Socrates is just demolishing opponents (the Thrasymachus set-to in Book 3, for example) in ways that also seem somewhat to justify Nietzsche's "resentful" observations. I think there are more than two "Platos," and perhaps that plurality of philosophical personae is both cause and effect of all Platonic occasions, re-presenting in one form or another, the most ancient of all philosophical problems—and the source of dialogue itself—the One and the Many.

Glossary

agapē [Greek]: selfless or disinterested love; contrast with *erōs* and *philia.*

agon [Greek]: contest or struggle, which can be physical, intellectual or aesthetic.

agora [Greek]: the central political and commercial gathering-place in ancient Greek cities.

aisthanesthai [Greek]: to perceive, to apprehend through the senses. The term etymologically provides the root for "aesthetics," suggesting that beauty is generated through sensuous apprehension.

aktive Vergesslichkeit [German]: active forgetting. This is Nietzsche's term for a repression of memory that can be both liberating and generative, especially for artists.

alētheia [Greek]: truth. In using this term, Heidegger emphasizes the etymology of the word *(a-lētheia)*, which literally means "not being hidden," "not being concealed." For Heidegger, "truth" is a matter neither of "correspondence" to a state of affairs nor of the internal "coherence" of a discourse, but of a "revelation" or "opening up" into "unconcealedness," in which the world discloses itself to and for human understanding.

Allzumenschlichkeit [German]: the state of being all-too-human. The word is drawn from Nietzsche's *Menschliches, Allzumenschliches* [*Human, All Too Human*].

amour courtois [French]: courtly love.

anagnōrisis [Greek]: recognition. Aristotle uses the term in *Poetics* to refer to the moment in Greek tragedy when the hero recognizes the truth of his situation (e.g. Oedipus realizes that he has killed his father and slept with his mother).

anamnēsis [Greek]: calling to mind, recollection. Plato theorized that learning is actually the process of remembering innate but forgotten knowledge; see Plato's *Meno*.

apophrades: [Latin]: literary-critical term from Harold Bloom's *The Anxiety of Influence*; this is the most radical of Bloom's so-called revisionary ratios, in which an author seeks to overcome the influence of the past by becoming his own precursor.

arête [Greek]: goodness, excellence, virtue, nobility, merit.

Aufhebung [German]: usually translated as "sublation," the word comes from the verb *aufheben*, which variously means "to cancel," "to preserve," "to lift up." Deriving from G. F. W. Hegel's philosophy, the term describes an historical process in which opposing ideas (a thesis and antithesis) enter into a conflict that simultaneously destroys and preserves elements of each idea, transforming these elements into a new and higher synthesis.

Bedeutung [German]: significance. A term from hermeneutics that refers to the significance a literary work has for a reader; *Bedeutung* is sometimes associated with anachronistic or subjective reading (what the text means *for me*, as opposed to what it means); see *Sinn*.

Bildung [German]: education, formation, growth, culture.

bovarysme [French]: given to a romantic fantasizing that often results in the denial of reality—as epitomized by Emma Bovary in Flaubert's *Madame Bovary*.

caritas [Latin]: distinterested love; also affection, esteem, charity (compare with *agapē*). According to Aquinas, *caritas* is the highest of the Christian virtues.

chronos [Greek]: ordinary or everyday time, time as it passes sequentially or chronologically; opposed to the revelatory time of *kairos*.

clinamen [Latin]: swerving aside. In Lucretius' *On the Nature of Things*, the swerving movement of atoms as they fall through the void. Harold Bloom uses the term in *The Anxiety of Influence* to indicate a canny swerving-away from the influence of a literary predecessor or tradition.

cogito [Latin]: a thinking or perceiving consciousness, as in the Cartesian subject, but the term is also sometimes used as shorthand for Descartes's "cogito ergo sum" [I think therefore I am].

"Das Ewige-Weibliche zieht uns hinan" [German]: from Goethe's *Faust*: "The Eternal-Feminine draws us onward."

Dasein [German]: a central concept in Heidegger's philosophy, *Dasein* replaces the abstract Cartesian *cogito* with a conception of the human being as radically immersed in the world, changing over time and mediated through engagements with objects, other people, language and mortality.

doxa [Greek]: common or accepted belief, opinion; as opposed to *epistēmē* [knowledge].

eidos [Greek]: form, essence, type. Refers to Plato's theory of forms, which posits an abstract realm of ideas immune to the flux of material reality.

eikasia [Greek]: likeness, image, conjecture. Refers in Plato to the realm of appearances as opposed to the ultimate reality of the *eidos*.

ekphrasis [Greek]: description; a rhetorical or literary device of extended description, especially one in which the language becomes so elaborate as to overwhelm the object being described; see Homer's description of the Shield of Achilles in *The Iliad*.

epistēmē [Greek]: knowledge; as opposed to *doxa* [opinion].

erōs [Greek]: passionate or sexual love. The term was used by Sigmund Freud to indicate the life-instinct as opposed to *thanatos*, which Freud associated with aggression, violence and the death-drive; see also *agapē* and *philia*.

Gesamtkunstwerk [German]: the total work of art; Wagner used the term to express his ideal of unifying the arts (music, literature, theatre and the visual arts) in his operatic works.

hamartia [Greek]: missing the mark, error in judgment. Aristotle uses this term in *Poetics* to describe the character flaw of the hero in Greek tragedy.

hoi polloi [Greek]: the many, the masses, the common people.

"Il se promène lisant au livre de lui-méme" [French]: "he walks reading in the book of himself." The quotation, drawn from Stéphane Mallarmé's "Hamlet et Fortinbras," refers to Hamlet; it is later cited in the "Scylla and Charybdis" episode of Joyce's *Ulysses*.

jenseits [German]: beyond. See Friedrich Nietzsche's *Jenseits von Gute und Böse* [*Beyond Good and Evil*].

jouissance [French]: sensual pleasure, orgasm, climax. Roland Barthes uses the word to indicate an aesthetic pleasure so sensuous that it is almost carnal.

kairos [Greek]: a significant or revelatory moment of elevated significance; opposed to the everyday time of *chronos*.

katharsis [Greek]: purification or cleansing. Aristotle uses the term in *Poetics* to refer to the therapeutic effect of tragedy, which is meant to purge the spectator's emotions, especially those of pity and fear.

le mot juste [French]: the right word. Flaubert would sometimes labor for days to find the most accurate and precise word to describe a character, action or situation.

logos [Greek]: word, speech, discourse, argument, reason, logic. It may be thought of as both cause and effect of an animating dialectic between two minds as they gain at once lucidity and understanding.

l'homme moyen sensuel [French]: the non-intellectual man of average tastes and feelings.

Menschenfrei [German]: free of people, without people.

nostos [Greek]: return or homecoming, especially after a long journey; often used to refer to Odysseus' return to Ithaca.

ostranenie [Russian]: defamiliarization. Viktor Shklovsky theorized that the significance of poetic language lies in its ability to break down (or defamiliarize) the reader's routine or habitualized perceptions of reality.

ousia [Greek]: being, essence, substance.

parousia [Greek]: physical presence or arrival. In Christian theology, the term refers to the second-coming (arrival) of Jesus.

peripatētikos [Greek]: the act of walking around, often teaching or conversing at the same time; refers to the so-called peripatetic school of philosophy associated with Aristotle; Socrates and Plato were also known to wander and discourse at the same time.

la petite mort [French]: the little death; a euphemism for sexual orgasm.

philia [Greek]: friendship or brotherly love; see *agapē* and *erōs*.

pithos [Greek]: a large jar or container used for storage. Refers to the cynic Diogenes, who is reputed to have taken such a jar as his home.

poêle [French]: stove. Refers to the stove-heated room in which Descartes formulated his famous dictum: "I think, therefore I am."

poiēsis [Greek]: making or bringing-forth; "poetry" derives from this word.

polis [Greek]: the ancient Greek city-state.

polytropos [Greek]: many-turns, many-forms, many-tropes. Homer uses this word to describe Odysseus as verbally facile and resourceful.

"*Post coitum omne animal triste est.*" [Latin]: Every animal is sad after coitus.

res cogitans [Latin]: thinking thing. The phrase was used by Descartes to refer to the subject; see also *cogito*.

ressentiment [French]: resentment. In *On the Genealogy of Morals*, Nietzsche theorized that Judeo-Christian morality arose out of the impotent hostility or resentment felt by the powerless toward the powerful.

Sein [German]: "Being" (as a noun) and "to be" (as a verb); see Heidegger's *Being and Time*.

Seinsfrage [German]: the question of Being; see Heidegger's *Being and Time*.

Sinn [German]: sense, meaning. In hermeneutics, this refers to the meaning of a literary text, its intentional design and structure, which the critic strives to uncover through close-reading combined with biographical and historical contextualization. *Sinn* is often opposed to *Bedeutung*, which refers not to the meaning of the text but to its "significance" for a reader.

stil novo [Italian]: new style. Refers to a literary movement from thirteenth-century Italy characterized by sophistication of expression and idealized representations of women and love.

stoa [Greek]: a covered walkway or portico.

Sturm und Drang [German]: storm and stress. A proto-Romantic movement in Germany characterized by subjective expression and tumultuous emotionalism.

tabula rasa [Latin]: blank slate. The term is associated with John Locke's epistemology, which argues that human knowledge is not innate but derives from perception and experience; compare with Plato's theory of knowledge-as-memory (see *anamnēsis*).

technē [Greek]: craftsmanship or art.

thanatos [Greek]: the death drive. Freud associated this term with the human propensity for aggression and violence.

to kalon [Greek]: beauty.

thumos [Greek]: high-spiritedness. In Homer, this quality is often associated with the temperament of the warrior.

Übermensch [German]: overman; often mistranslated as Superman, with all the comic-book overtones that carries. The word particularly refers to Nietzsche's conception of a "higher spirit" whose strength of will transvalues all values in an act of creative freedom.

Ubi saeva indignatio / Ulterius cor lacerare nequit [Latin]: Where savage indignation is no longer able to lacerate his heart.

unzeitgemäss [German]: out-of-fashion. See Friedrich Nietzsche's *Unzeitgemässe Betrachtungen* or *Untimely Meditations.*

unzeitig [German]: unseasonable, untimely.

Verfremdungseffekt [German]: estrangement-effect or alienation-effect. So named by Bertolt Brecht, this dramatic device is designed to break up or disrupt the theatrical illusion-of-reality by reminding the audience that they are simply watching a play.

Vergessenheit [German]: oblivion.

Vergesslichkeit [German]: forgetfulness.

Vorstellung [German]: representation.

vulgus [Latin]: the people, the multitude, the public.

Weltschmerz [German]: world-weariness.

Zeitlichkeit [German]: temporality; associated with Heidegger's idea of Being-in-time.

Zweckmässigkeit ohne Zweck [German]: Purposiveness without purpose. In Immanuel Kant's aesthetics, the term indicates that although the work of art has design—it was "purposively" constructed by the artist—it nevertheless has no "purpose" in the sense of a practical function in the world. In other words, art is "autonomous"—not a means but an end-in-itself—and therefore the pleasure one derives from it is "disinterested." See Kant's *Critique of Judgment.*

Index

Achebe, Chinua 31, 32
Adams, John 159
Adorno, Theodor 9, 19, 52, 55, 151
Allen, Woody 87
Anselm (of Canterbury) 125
Aquinas, Thomas 173, 178
Arendt, Hannah 63
Aristophanes 104
Aristotle 26, 28, 30, 132, 166, 167, 177, 181
Arnold, Matthew 18, 26
Auden, W.H. 132
Auerbach, Erich 35, 38, 39, 53
Augustine (of Hippo) 102, 171
Austen, Jane 22, 31

Barnes, Julian 3
Barthes, Roland 7, 19, 38, 180
Bataille, Georges 67
Baudelaire, Charles 7, 9, 12, 60, 66, 77, 90
Beckett, Samuel xi, xiii, 5, 11, 12, 22, 72, 81, 85, 86, 88, 92, 132, 133, 138, 139, 153
Beethoven, Ludwig van 21, 25, 27, 32, 152
Benjamin, Walter 16, 17, 19, 35, 37, 40, 45, 52, 53, 55
Berkeley, George x
Blake, William 9, 60, 68
Bloom, Allan 115, 160
Bloom, Harold 68, 145, 146, 148, 149, 151, 158, 178
Boethius x
Bolaño, Roberto 121
Bonaparte, Napolean 62, 152
Borges, Jorge Luis 134, 135
Brando, Marlon 101
Brecht, Bertolt 43, 52, 92, 183
Brod, Max 77
Brontë, Emily 67
Browning, Robert 100
Burke, Edmund 66
Burns, Robert 6
Burroughs, William 21
Bush, George W. 109, 115, 116
Byron, George Gordon 5, 17, 60, 68, 82, 90, 91, 115, 121, 130, 131, 138, 139, 140, 152, 153, 154, 171

Camus, Albert 81, 82, 83, 88, 93, 136
Cantor, Paul 137
Čapek, Karel 90
Carlyle, Thomas 158
Celan, Paul 75, 77, 78
Céline, Louis-Ferdinand 22

Chaucer, Geoffrey 102, 143
Churchill, Winston 129
Clinton, Hillary 113
Colet, Louise 4, 87
Conrad, Joseph xi, 32, 60, 63, 64, 65, 66, 67, 68, 69, 70, 77, 78, 79, 80, 115, 168
Copernicus, Nicolaus 127
Croff, Giuseppe 37, 39, 40, 49, 51, 52

Dante, Allighieri 22, 60, 71, 96, 97, 104, 105
Danto, Arthur 47
Darwin, Charles 96, 97, 104
Darwin, Emma 96, 97
Defoe, Daniel 6
de Nerval, Gérard 108
Derrida, Jacques xi, 19, 38, 115, 168, 172, 173, 174
Descartes, René xi, 125, 126, 127, 128, 129, 131, 132, 133, 134, 135, 136, 137, 138, 139, 140, 179, 181
Dewey, John 113, 115
Dickens, Charles 50
Dickinson, Emily 132, 133, 161
Diogenes 131, 132, 133, 135, 136, 181
Dostoyevsky, Fyodor 60
Duchamp, Marcel 9, 45, 47
du Mauriers, Daphne 106
Durrell, Lawrence 121

Eagleton, Terry 24
Ehrenpreis, Irvin 23
Eichmann, Adolph 64, 65, 70, 78, 79
Eliot, T.S. 13, 14, 22, 32, 43, 66, 111, 117, 142, 143, 148, 149, 151
Emerson, Ralph Waldo 143, 150
Emin, Tracey 9, 17, 47

Faulkner, William 111, 121
Fénelon, François x
Fey, Tina 35, 51
Fish, Stanley 68
Fitzgerald, F. Scott 20
Flaubert, Gustave x, 3, 4, 17, 31, 49, 50, 87, 111, 132, 133, 178, 180
Ford, Henry 95
Forster, E.M. 130
Foucault, Michel 19
Freud, Sigmund 99

Gadamer, Hans-Georg 25
Galilei, Galileo 125, 126, 127, 129
Gardner, John 61
Giotto (di Bordone) 103
Goebbels, Joseph 73
Goethe, Johann Wolfgang von 28, 50, 60, 75, 152, 179
Goldhagen, Daniel 73
Gore, Al 113
Gray, John 60
Greenberg, Clement 49
Gwaltney, P.D. 108

Hardy, Thomas 22
Harvey, William 127
Hassan, Ihab 18, 20, 27, 34
Hawking, Stephen 103
Hegel, Georg Wilhelm Friedrich 133
Heidegger, Martin xi, xii, 9, 11, 40, 43, 82, 83, 89, 132, 138, 154, 155, 156, 157, 158, 177, 179, 182, 183
Henderson, Nevile 54
Heraclitus 103, 166
Himmler, Heinrich 63, 71, 73
Hirsch, E.D. 24
Hitler, Adolf 22, 35, 53, 55, 59, 62, 73
Hobbes, Thomas 71, 75, 80
Homer 8, 12, 13, 22, 23, 29, 35, 55, 69, 93, 98, 134, 152, 167, 179, 182
Horace 29, 132
Hrabal, Bohumil 111

Iser, Wolfgang 19

James, Henry 7, 111
Janáček, Leoš 90
Jefferson, Thomas 114, 121, 122, 128, 130, 159, 161, 175
Johnson, Samuel 51, 81, 100, 103, 146, 147
Joyce, James 13, 20, 22, 33, 52, 69, 86, 109, 115, 142, 144, 145, 148, 149, 151, 153, 180

Kafka, Franz 60, 77
Kant, Immanuel 5, 20, 30, 55, 69, 71, 74, 92, 102, 121, 128, 149, 183
Keats, John 14, 87
Kermode, Frank 37, 38, 85
Kertész, Imre 77
Kierkegaard, Søren 150, 151, 154
Kracauer, Siegfried 55
Kubrick, Stanley 55
Kundera, Milan 102, 103
Kyd, Thomas 143

Lacan, Jacques 36, 37, 106, 171
Landor, Walter Savage x
Larkin, Philip 59, 74, 79
La Rochefoucauld, François de 4
Lawrence, D.H. 75
Levenson, Michael 32, 70, 80
Levi, Primo 77
Lewis, Wyndham 22
Locke, John 150, 182
London, Jack 133
Longinus 29
Lucretius 83, 99, 178
Lukács, Georg 16
Luther, Martin 128, 129
Lysippos 85

Machiavelli, Niccolò 137
Mailer, Norman 21
Malebranche, Nicolas x
Mallarmé, Stéphane 81, 180
Mann, Thomas 153
Mapplethorpe, Robert 8

Marlowe, Christopher 21, 22
Matisse, Henri 31
Max, Peter 49
McCarthy, Cormac 79, 80
McClary, Susan 24, 27
McGann, Jerome 21, 22, 24
Milton, John 22, 60, 69, 129
Monet, Claude 92
Montaigne, Michel de 82, 136, 137
Mozart, Wolfgang Amadeus 20, 51, 52, 92, 151, 152
Muni, Paul 35, 52
Murdoch, Iris x
Mussolini, Benito 22

Nabokov, Vladimir 30, 110, 111, 121
Nietzsche, Friedrich xi, 19, 28, 35, 63, 64, 66, 72, 75, 78, 81, 83, 93, 95, 98, 111, 115, 117, 134, 138, 141, 143, 144, 148, 149, 150, 151, 152, 154, 155, 156, 158, 173, 174, 176, 177, 183

Obama, Barack 113, 115, 116, 160
O'Connor, Flannery 76

Parmenides 135, 166
Pater, Walter 44, 92, 93
Paul (the Apostle) 104, 137, 171
Petrarch, Francesco 96, 104, 106
Petronius 45
Picasso, Pablo 31, 50, 72, 103
Pindar 135
Plato xi, xii, xiii, 9, 19, 26, 28, 30, 36, 83, 96, 97, 98, 103, 105, 115, 121, 131, 132, 134, 135, 150, 151, 152, 153, 155, 156, 157, 176, 183
Plotinus 171
Pope, Alexander 64, 120
Popper, Karl 160
Pound, Ezra 9, 23, 24, 26, 32, 50, 111
Protagoras 166
Proust, Marcel 13, 21, 60, 121, 153

Rabelais, François 4
Rancière, Jacques 6
Ranke, Leopold von 149
Riefenstahl, Leni 54, 55
Rimbaud, Arthur 21, 84
Rorty, Richard xi, xii, 21, 112, 118, 138
Roscoe, William 122
Rosen, Charles 25
Rousseau, Jean-Jacques 71, 74, 80
Rushdie, Salman 66
Ruskin, John 44

Sade, Donatien de 8, 67
Sainte-Beuve, Charles Augustin 105
Santayana, George x, 150
Sartre, Jean-Paul 93, 113
Schlesinger, Elisa 87
Schneemann, Carolee 8
Schneider, Maria 101

Schopenhauer, Arthur 97
Sedgwick, Eve Kosofsky 22, 24
Seneca 82
Shakespeare, William xi, 21, 22, 60, 76, 82, 86, 87, 89, 103, 115, 116, 133, 134, 135, 137, 139, 145, 147, 160
Shaw, George Bernard 31, 106
Shelley, Mary 61
Shelley, Percy Byshe 61
Shklovsky, Viktor 30, 92, 181
Shostakovich, Dmitri 13
Socrates xiii, 11, 28, 106, 112, 132, 134, 135, 150, 152, 176, 181
Sontag, Susan 106
Sophocles 27, 60
Speer, Albert 53, 54
Stalin, Joseph 59, 79
Steiner, George 26, 28
Stevens, Wallace 105, 107, 111, 163
Stoppard, Tom 139
Strauss, Leo 160
Stravinsky, Igor 50
Swift, Jonathan 74, 122

Tanner, Tony 31
Tennyson, Alfred 22, 87
Thales 138, 157
Tolstoy, Leo 84, 89
Trilling, Lionel 19, 21

Updike, John 4, 79

Van Gogh, Vincent 9, 11, 12, 93
Verlaine, Paul 21
Villon, François 21
Vinci, Leonardo da 37
Virgil 14, 22, 69
Vlaminck, Maurice de 32
Voeglin, Eric 160
Voltaire 4, 50

Wagner, Richard 152, 179
Warhol, Andy 4, 8, 12, 15, 47, 49, 51
Washington, George 109
Whitman, Walt 14, 113, 115, 122
Wiesel, Elie 77
Wilde, Oscar x, 27, 60, 61, 62, 118, 131
Williams, Bernard 90
Wittgenstein, Ludwig xi, 30, 43, 158, 170
Woods, Tiger 119
Woolf, Virginia 35, 103, 153
Wordsworth, William 5, 18, 22, 91, 92, 93, 142, 152, 153, 155, 156, 157, 158

Xenophon x

Yeats, W.B. 22, 75

About the Authors

RICHARD BEGAM is Professor of English at the University of Wisconsin-Madison and has been a Visiting Professor at Duke University, the University of Düsseldorf and Stockholm University. He is the author of *Samuel Beckett and the End of Modernity* (Stanford University Press, 1996) and co-editor of *Modernism and Colonialism* (Duke University Press, 2007), *Text and Meaning* (Düsseldorf University Press, 2010) and *Modernism, Postcolonialism and Globalism* (Oxford University Press, forthcoming). He is finishing a book entitled *Beckett's Philosophical Levity*.
ORCID: 0000-0001-5411-8272

JAMES SODERHOLM has published *Fantasy, Forgery and the Byron Legend* (University Press of Kentucky, 1997), *Beauty and the Critic: Aesthetics in an Age of Cultural Studies* (University of Alabama Press, 1998) and *Byron and Romanticism* (Cambridge University Press, 2002). He has taught literature and aesthetics at the University of Wisconsin-Milwaukee, Baylor University, Charles University in Prague and The King's School in Canterbury. He is currently Professor of Humanities at Simon Langton Grammar School for Boys in Canterbury. He is writing a book on Hamlet.
ORCID: 0000-0003-0477-3636

www.ingramcontent.com/pod-product-compliance
Lightning Source LLC
LaVergne TN
LVHW010901110826
845149LV00005B/1435